The Songs of Squeezing Out Sparks

As recorded by Graham Parker and The Rumour

40th Anniversary Edition

Compiled by Martin Belmont

Tangible press

Copyright © 2019 Martin Belmont

Published by Tangible Press
www.tangiblepress.net

All rights reserved. This book or any portion thereof may not be reproduced or used in any manner whatsoever without the express written permission of the publisher except for the use of brief quotations in a book review.

ISBN-13: 978-1-7323892-7-4
ISBN-10: 1-7323892-7-6

Book design by Martin Belmont and John Howells

Cover design and art by Jimmy Parker

Notation and tablature written using TablEdit
www.tabledit.com

Photographs:

Pages 4, 5, 6, 7, 60 (bottom), 61 (upper right), 61 (bottom): Bruce Dinsmor

Additional photography by Jolie Parker

All songs, except "I Want You Back (Alive)", written by Graham Parker
Published by Ellisclan Ltd.,
All rights administered by BMG Rights Management (US) LLC

"I Want You Back (Alive)" by The Corporation
(Berry Gordy, Freddie Perren, Alphonso Mizell, Deke Richards)
Jobete Music Co Inc.

CONTENTS

Introduction 4

Reading the Song Sheets 8

Tab Key 9

Song Index 10

INTRODUCTION

After producing the excellent book, "The Songs Of Three Chords Good and Mystery Glue", Martin Belmont has now turned his highly skilled attentions to Squeezing Out Sparks. On one of our regular get-togethers over an Indian meal, Martin mentioned that Squeezing Out Sparks will be 40 years old in 2019, which is as good an excuse as you'd need to publish an SOS song book.

Brinsley was brought in to go over his parts so Martin could notate and tab them. Now this was an album which was released in March 1979. Yes, there was much head scratching going on as they tried to figure out just what the hell they'd been playing all those years ago. It's typical that musicians who make an album, then go out on tour where they will play some of those songs, will change what they play very quickly, and often from night to night, to make the songs more suitable in a live setting. The parts they play are constantly morphing, so it's often baffling to revisit the original form of any particular record. My job was easy - I played very little guitar on Sparks and merely had to proof read the lyrics!

Graham Parker

Squeezing Out Sparks is an album with a production and arrangements that favour the guitars alongside the drums and bass behind Graham's vocal. Unlike previous GP&TR albums there are no horns, no strings and less prominent keyboards. In many ways, for all its riches and its stellar reputation, the album is a bit of an anomaly. No other GP&TR record sounds anything like it! That's why I decided to take a more comprehensive approach to the guitar tab/notation. Eight songs have Brinsley's part from start to finish, including the solos - unlike the previous songbook which just had the intro riffs, a little melodic hook here and there or an acoustic picking interlude.

Three of those eight songs have Brinsley's part AND mine from start to finish. All of this took a lot of work, figuring out what exactly we played and transcribing the notation and tablature. Brinsley's contribution was enormous both in travel time and hours spent working on the songs. So many days we planned to get through two or three songs and ended up totally knackered after completing just one!

Martin Belmont

p.s The original Squeezing Out Sparks had ten songs. However, recorded around the same time and released as a stand alone single were 'Mercury Poisoning' and 'I Want You Back' and they have since been added to every re-release of the album, so they are included in this collection.

During the thirty odd years from 1981 to 2016 I spent a good deal of my time working as a guitar repairer. During that time hundreds of guitar players told me what they thought was wrong with their guitar and amp sound. A frequent comment was 'it just doesn't sound like the sound I have in my head'. I now realise that this was something I also suffered from for years. What I could hear was a cross between Hank Marvin and Robbie Robertson, lovely clean big floating sustain but with a biting dangerous edge.

When The Rumour began in 1975 I had a 1963 Fender Jazzmaster, because it cost just £75, and an old Twin Reverb, because it was loud. Not a combination that readily gave up that big singing gritty sound I had in my head. Then I bought an MXR Dynacomp Compressor pedal and it became such a key part of my sound that I had the guts of it installed inside my Jazzmaster! This was as close as I could get to what I wanted, and I was happy...

Sometime later, while wandering the streets of San Francisco in search of a quiet beer, I came across a guitar store. In the window was an old Gibson Flying V. I had to go and try it and really liked it so I bought it. It had nothing to do with the "sound in my head", but it was great fun to play. Squeezing Out Sparks was the first album I used it on. It seemed to fit perfectly, on Protection and Nobody Hurts You for example, working really well alongside Martin's newly acquired Gretsch Branding Iron. Playing the Flying V on Squeezing Out Sparks was a defining moment for me. It changed me as a guitarist. Later, touring in England, we played Hammersmith Odeon, and Dave Edmunds dropped in to our soundcheck. Excited to show him my fab new guitar I dragged him on stage and played him a bit. 'Isn't it great' I prompted. 'Yeah' he replied nonchalantly, 'but you sound just like you always do'. Which, I realised later, could have been a compliment!

Brinsley Schwarz

THE GUITARS

Brinsley plays the Gibson Flying V on Discovering Japan, Local Girls, Nobody Hurts You, Passion Is No Ordinary Word, Saturday Nite Is Dead (just the solo), Love Gets You Twisted, Protection and Don't Get Excited.

The Fender Jazzmaster is used on Saturday Nite Is Dead, Waiting For The UFO's, Mercury Poisoning and I Want You Back.

Martin plays the Gretsch Branding Iron on Discovering Japan, Local Girls, Nobody Hurts You, Love Gets You Twisted, Protection, Don't Get Excited.

The Fender Stratocaster is played on Passion Is No Ordinary Word, I Want You Back and a Gibson L6 on Mercury Poisoning and Saturday Nite Is Dead.

Graham plays a Guild D45 acoustic on You Can't Be Too Strong, Passion, Love Gets You Twisted and UFO's. He also played a Gibson ES-330 on a couple of other tracks.

READING THE SONGSHEETS

2/4   Time signatures (Usually for the whole song but sometimes
4/4   just for one bar when indicated)

/   Bar line

D7 Chord

//: Indicates the start of a section to be repeated

:// The point where you return to the start of a section and repeat it.

N.C No chord

\>   Accent on the beat (anticipated/pushed beat)

1 & 2 & 3 & Rhythm riff (Don't Get Excited)
| | | | | |

TAB KEY

SONG INDEX

Discovering Japan
Lyrics & Chords, Main riffs tab
(page 14)

Local Girls
Lyrics & Chords, Intro & Chorus riffs tab
(page 19)

Nobody Hurts You
Lyrics & Chords, Complete lead guitar tab
(page 25)

You Can't Be Too Strong
Lyrics & Chords, Chord window, Acoustic guitar riffs tab
(page 37)

Passion Is No Ordinary Word
Lyrics & Chords, Complete lead guitar tab
(page 41)

Saturday Nite Is Dead
Lyrics & Chords, Complete lead guitar tab
(page 63)

Love Gets You Twisted
Lyrics & Chords, Complete lead guitar tab
(page 78)

Protection
Lyrics & Chords, Complete lead & rhythm guitar tabs
(page 85)

Waiting For The Ufos
Lyrics & Chords, Complete lead guitar tab
(page 114)

Don't Get Excited
Lyrics & Chords, Complete lead & rhythm guitar tabs
(page 122)

Mercury Poisoning
Lyrics & Chords, Rhythm guitar intro tab
(page 148)

I Want You Back (Alive)
Lyrics & Chords, Complete lead & rhythm guitar tabs
(page 151)

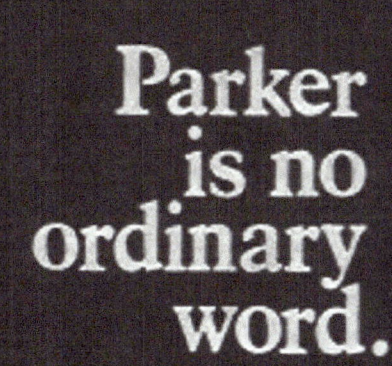

Parker is no ordinary word.

And neither are the words used to describe his new album, Graham Parker's SQUEEZING OUT SPARKS. The VILLAGE VOICE gave it an "A−," calling it "an amazing record," ROLLING STONE called it "as explosive a piece of rock & roll as we are likely to hear this year." And, the LOS ANGELES TIMES hailed Parker as "the most compelling rock figure to emerge in the 1970's."

Graham Parker's SQUEEZING OUT SPARKS. On Arista Records and Tapes.

ARISTA

Produced by Jack Nitzsche
for North Spur Productions Inc.
Recorded and mixed by Mark Howlett.

Still the 334th greatest album of all time according to Rolling Stone's top 500 albums as listed in 2013

RELEASED MARCH 1979

GRAHAM PARKER: LEAD VOCALS, RHYTHM GUITAR
BRINSLEY SCHWARZ: GUITAR AND BACKING VOCALS
MARTIN BELMONT: RHYTHM GUITAR AND BACKING VOCALS
BOB ANDREWS: KEYBOARDS AND BACKING VOCALS
STEVE GOULDING: DRUMS AND BACKING VOCALS
ANDREW BODNAR: BASS

PRODUCER: JACK NITZSCHE
ENGINEER: MARK HOWLETT
STUDIO ASSISTANT: PHIL BODGER

RECORDED AT LANSDOWNE STUDIOS, LONDON
MIXED AT CHEROKEE STUDIOS, HOLLYWOOD
MASTERED AT CRYSTAL INC., HOLLYWOOD,
BY MARK HOWLETT AND JEFF SANDERS

ALL SONGS WRITTEN BY GRAHAM PARKER
©1979 INTERSONG INC.

#75 IN ROLLING STONE'S LIST OF THE TOP 100 ALBUMS OF 1979

#45 IN ROLLING STONE'S LIST OF THE BEST ALBUMS OF THE LAST 20 YEARS (1967-1987)

#6 IN THE CREEM READER'S POLL 1979

VOTED ALBUM OF THE YEAR BY THE VILLAGE VOICE "PAZZ AND JOP" CRITICS POLL 1979

Squeezing Out Sparks was released in March 1979 on Vertigo Records in the UK and on Arista Records in the US. It was greeted with almost universal acclaim. Here are some of the reactions from critics:

Graham Parker and The Rumour are a great band – great meaning GREAT, not just quite-good-on-their-night or whatever. Passion is no ordinary word. Graham Parker's is no ordinary passion.

© Charles Shaar Murray, *New Musical Express* 1979

Squeezing Out Sparks, produced by former Phil Spector arranger Jack "Lonely Surfer" Nitzsche, lets you hear what Parker was after on *Stick to Me*, for it's made in the same vein, though this time the music is full of presence: turn the record up and it gets more exciting, not more shrill. In 1977, Graham Parker and the Rumour were reaching for the harshest edge in their music, and that's what they offer here. They've put aside the grandeur and the richness — horns, keyboards and the romantic pessimism — of the first two albums in favor of fuzz tone, fast tempos, hard drumming and desperate, even paranoid singing. The proof of the band's depth is that this approach is most successful at its most extreme.

© Greil Marcus, *Rolling Stone* 1979

When you play this album for perhaps the tenth time, when you return to 'You Can't Be Too Strong' and listen to that one song again and again until you no longer experience a fearful horror but complete sympathy — then you will understand that you've heard something quite extraordinary.

And if Graham Parker isn't the British artist of the decade, then he's certainly the most convincing manifestation of the '70s rock conscience to emerge so far.

Few albums have moved me like this one

© Tony Stewart, *New Musical Express*, 17 March 1979

DISCOVERING JAPAN
4/4

INTRO RIFF (see tab)

Pause	Pause	Pause		
Bm	/D	/Asus2	/	/
Pause	Pause	Pause		
Bm	/D	/Asus2	/	/
Pause	Pause	Pause		
Bm	/D	/Asus2	/	/

VERSE 1

```
D              /             /        /Bm           /
   Her heart is nearly breaking,  the earth is nearly quaking

D              /             /        /A            /
   The Tokyo   taxi's braking,    it's screaming to a halt

G              /A       /Bm           /G            /
   and there's nothing to hold on to     when gravity betrays you

A              /             /D           /Bm       /
   And every kiss enslaves you-oooooo - oooooooh

D              /             /        /Bm           /
   She knows how hard a heart grows      under the  nuclear shadows

D              /             /        /A            /
   She can't escape the feeling    repeating  in her head

G              /A       /Bm           /G            /
   When after all the urges     some kind of truth emerges

A              /       /Bm     A      /
   We felt the deadly surges Discovering   Ja-
```

CHORUS

```
G             / D        /Asus2       /            /
-pa----------------an                    Discovering   Ja-

G             /D         /Asus2       /            /
-pa----------------an
```

RIFF AFTER 1st CHORUS (see tab)
```
                    STOP
Bm          /                    /
```

VERSE 2

```
D          /        /       /Bm            /
   The GIs only used her.   They always ran right through her.

D          /        /           /A         /
   Giving an eastern promise, that they could never keep

G          /A         ./Bm           /G           /
   Seeing a million miles,    between their jokes and smiles

A          /          /D           /
   she heard their hard deni---------als
```

BRIDGE

```
Bm          /             /A          /             /
As the tears drop sideways down her face,       face

Bm          /             /A          /             /
I wake up talking in the tongue of a different race,    race    and as the

Bm          /             /G          /             /
flight touches down my watch says eight O two   but that's midnight   to
```

RIFF AFTER BRIDGE (see tab)

```
Bm              /D        /Asus2          /             /
you,                                          Midnight to


Bm              /D        /Asus2          /             /
you                                           Midnight to


Bm              /D        /Asus2          /             /
you


G               /A               //
```

VERSE 3

```
D            /              /          /Bm            /
   I dreamed headlong collisions    in jet lag panavisions

D            /              /          /A             /
   I shouted 'sayonara'            it didn't mean goodbye

G         /A         /Bm           /G              /
   But lovers turn to posers    show up in film exposures

A            /              /Bm    A  /
   Just like in travel brochures Discovering Ja
```

INTRO RIFF (see tab)

```
G           /D            /Asus2          /G              /
pa---------------a-----------------an      Discovering   Japa--------------

D           /Asus2         /           /G          /D             /
a----------------an         Discovering   Japa--------------a-----------------

Asus2         /         /G          /D              /
an              Discovering   Japa-------------------a-----------------

Asus2         /         /G          /D              /
an              Discovering   Japa-------------------a-----------------
```

SLOW FADE

DISCOVERING JAPAN
MAIN RIFFS

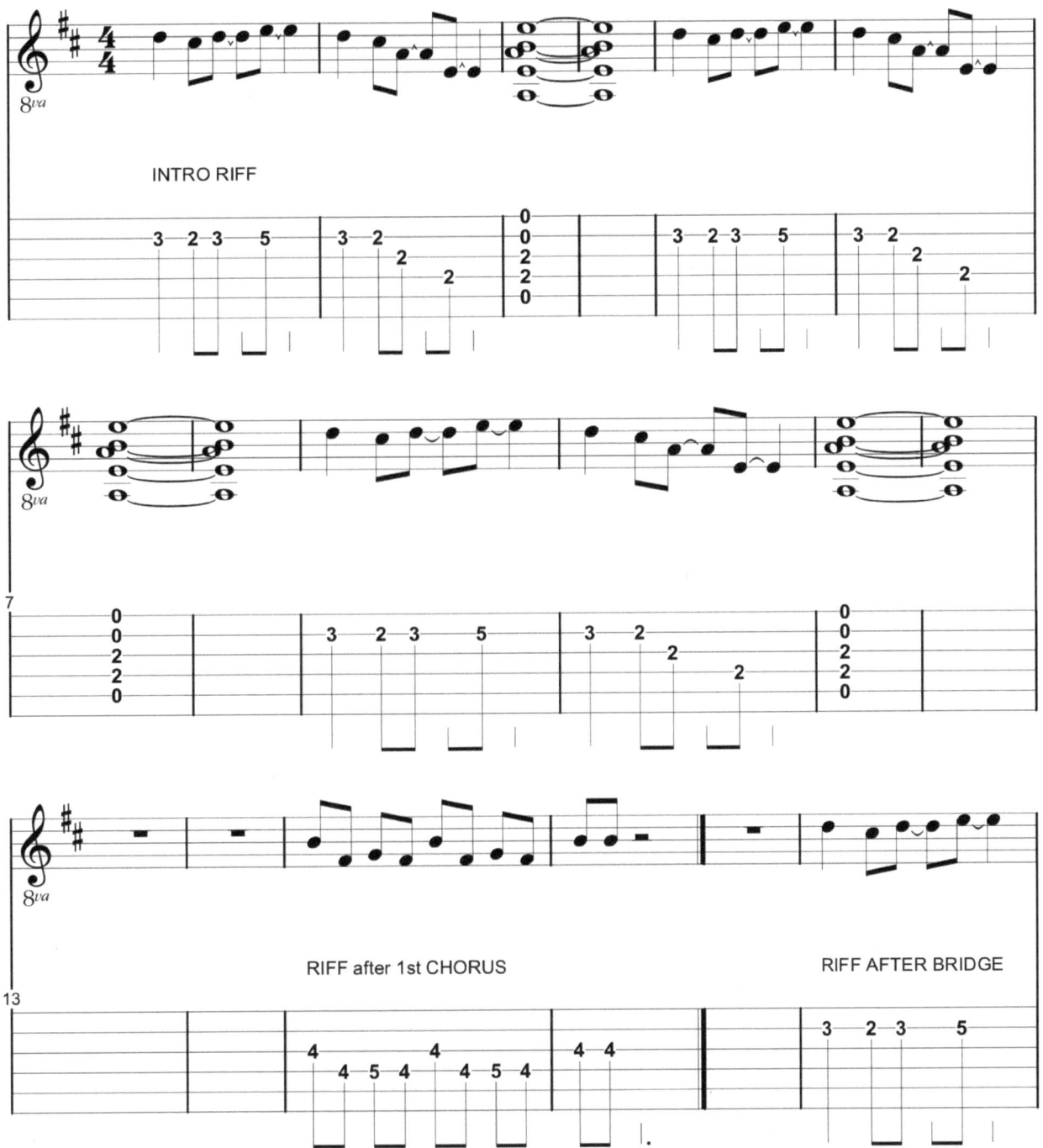

DISCOVERING JAPAN - MAIN RIFFS

LOCAL GIRLS

4/4

INTRO RIFF (see tab)

| D | /Bm G | /D | /Bm G | / |
| D | /Bm G | /G A | / |

VERSES 1 & 2

//:B   /E   /A   /G#m   E   /
   Sit by my window and look outside   Wonder why her sun don't shine on me
   She's probably halfwit she must be straight   Bound to have a mother who knows   nothing but hate

B   /E   /A   /G#m   C#   /
   What's wrong with you, you stupid child   Don't you think that I'm the one you're waiting to see
   Don't want her love I'd rather knock her down Standing at the bus stop where she waits each morning

F#   /Bm   /D   /E   /
Don't talk too much cause she falls for the soft touch Makes her feel everything is secure   Don't
So isolated that she   thinks   that the army is the place where a man ought to be   Don't

G   A   /
ever leave a footprint on her
bother with them they don't bother

CHORUS 1st time only (see tab)

D   /Bm   G   /D   /Bm   G   /
floor. Don't bother with the   local girls   Don't bother with the   local girls

D   /Bm   G   /G   A   ://
   Don't bother with the   local girls

CHORUS 2nd time (see tab)

D   /Bm   G   /D   /Bm   G   /
me. Don't bother with the   local girls   Don't bother with the   local girls

                                                            PAUSE
D   /Bm   G   /D   /G   /
   Don't bother with the   local girls   Don't bother with the   local girls. They

BRIDGE

```
A              /G            /A           /G            /
got  the walk  they got  the talk  right down  without a flaw         At

A              /G            /            A            /
six  o'clock   I got  to stop   my dreaming at the counter of the
```

INTRO RIFF (see tab)
```
D              /Bm     G      /D             /Bm    G    /
store (Don't bother with them)

D              /Bm     G     /G     A    //
```

VERSE 3
Without a doubt I got to intercept. Must be time someone went and shouted in their ear (Hey!)
You look all right in that cheap print dress but every time you swish it round you make me disappear
Yes I'm aware of exactly what I'm doing making everything a mystery
Don't bother with it, it don't bother

CHORUS 3 & OUTRO (see tab)
```
D                    /Bm    G    /D                    /Bm    G    /
me.  Don't bother with the   local girls     Don't bother with the   local girls

D                    /Bm    G    /G     A         /
    Don't bother with the   local girls don't bother with them they don't bother

D                    /Bm    G    /D                    /Bm    G    /
me  Don't bother with the   local girls     Don't bother with the   local girls
```

(SLOW FADE)
```
D                    /Bm    G    /G     A         /
    Don't bother with the   local girls don't bother bother bother bother

D                    /Bm    G    /D                    /Bm    G    /
    Don't bother with the   local girls     Don't bother with the   local girls

D                    /Bm    G    /G     A         /
    Don't bother with the   local girls don't bother with them they don't bother

D                         /
me
```

LOCAL GIRLS
INTRO & CHORUS RIFFS

LOCAL GIRLS - INTRO & CHORUS RIFFS

LOCAL GIRLS - INTRO & CHORUS RIFFS

23

NOBODY HURTS YOU

4/4

INTRO
```
Bm    E   A   /           /Bm    E   A   /           /
                    Pause……………….Pause………………
Bm    E   A   /           /D              /E         /
```

VERSE 1 & 2
```
//:G              /A              /D              /
```
I try to pull my weight, study my geography   It doesn't seem to get me anywhere
I once had respect,   woke up with the Daily News   and it looked like forever

```
G                 /A              /D              /
```
I hold a picture up, everybody thinks it's me   I get a thrill out of tamp'ring with the atmosphere
I had a coffee fix, every item there to choose all my love came by letter

```
Bm        /G          /Bm             /G      D   /
```
Hey baby, I'm   out of favour   You can't always be   the right flavour
Suffocating   in suburbia   The new estates build   claustrophobia

```
G                 /A              /              /
```
It just seems that no matter what you do   someone somewhere, somehow gotta punish you
Playing blind man's bluff loaded on the vital stuff   that's enough that's enough   that's enough well

CHORUS 1 & 2
```
D         /Asus   A   /G              /A              /
```
Nobody hurts you,   nobody hurts you   Well
                                                    Pause……………..
```
D         /Asus   A   /Bm             /G A            /
```
Nobody hurts you,   nobody hurts you   Harder than your

```
G                 /D              /A              /
```
self,   harder than yourself   Harder than your

```
G                 /D              /A              :// 
```
self,   harder than yourself

INTRO

VERSE 3
You make me tag along, run into the rent-a-crowd but they're just imitation
I try to write the song, you and me are laughing loud but it comes out frustration
Look, no one's going to illuminate you. All the odds are stacked against you.
You're just caving in right there in front of me, it's a picture I don't ever want to see

CHORUS 3

```
D                /Asus    A    /G                /A                    /
Nobody hurts you,              nobody hurts you                    Well
                                                        Pause....................
D                /Asus    A    /Bm               /G A                  /
Nobody hurts you,              nobody hurts you        Harder than your
```

CRESCENDO

QUIETLY..
```
G(One short chord)  /(One short chord)    /D(One short chord) /A(One short chord)   /
self,                  harder than yourself                Harder than your
```

A LITTLE LOUDER...
```
G(One short chord)  /(One short chord)    /D(One short chord) /A(One short chord)   /
self,                  harder than yourself                Harder than your
```

A LITTLE MORE LOUDER...
```
G(One short chord)  /(One short chord)    /D(One short chord) /A(One short chord)   /
self,                  harder than yourself                Harder than your
```

STILL LOUDER!!..
```
G(One short chord)  /(One short chord)    /D(One short chord) /A(One short chord)   /
self,                  harder than yourself                         Well

G                  /              /D                /A                    /
Nobody hurts you                  Nobody hurts you

G                  /              /D                /A                    /
Nobody hurts you                  Nobody hurts you   Harder than your

G                  /              /D                /A                    /
self,               harder than yourself              Harder than your

G                  /              /D                /A                    /
self,               harder than yourself                Well well well

G                  /              /D                /A                    /
Nobody hurts you                  Nobody hurts you

G                  /              /D                /A                    /
Nobody hurts you                  Nobody hurts you
          >
G..........G.....G
Nobody hurts you
```

NOBODY HURTS YOU
LEAD GUITAR

NOBODY HURTS YOU - LEAD GUITAR

NOBODY HURTS YOU - LEAD GUITAR

30

NOBODY HURTS YOU - LEAD GUITAR

VERSE 3

NOBODY HURTS YOU - LEAD GUITAR

CRESCENDO

NOBODY HURTS YOU - LEAD GUITAR

END CRESCENDO

OUTRO

NOBODY HURTS YOU - LEAD GUITAR

NOBODY HURTS YOU - LEAD GUITAR

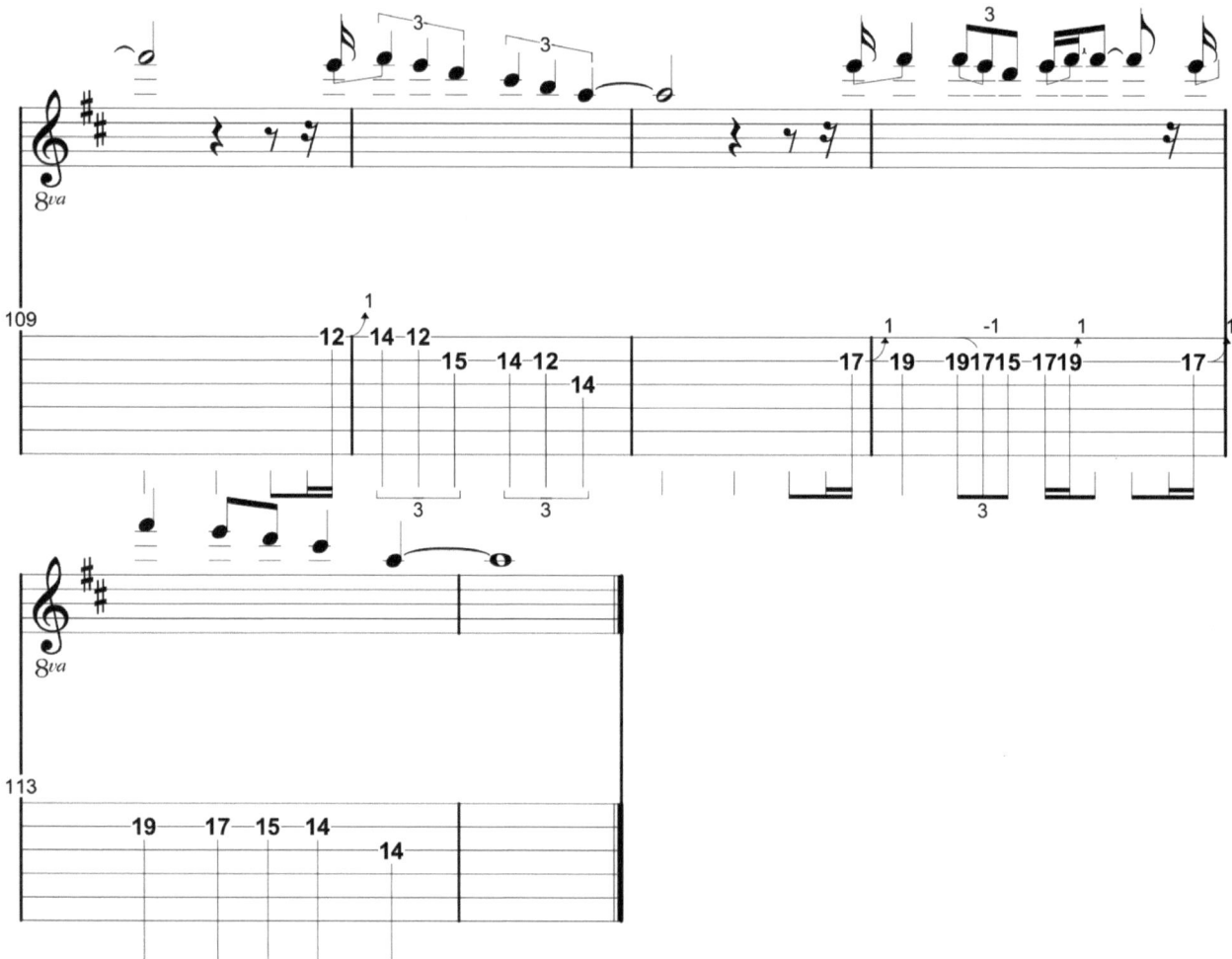

YOU CAN'T BE TOO STRONG 4/4

INTRO (see tab)

| E | /Badd4 | /E | /Aadd2 | / |

| E | /Badd4 | / |

```
//:E            /B              /C#m            /G#m            /
    Did they tear it out  with talons of steel   and give you a shot,  so that you wouldn't
    Well I ain't gonna cry,    I'm gonna rejoice and shout myself dry and go see the
                    .........RIFF BARS 13 & 14 (see tab)...............
A            /B              /E              /Aadd2    Badd4    /
feel? and washed it away    as if it wasn't real?
boys they'll laugh when I say    I left it overseas

E            /B              /C#m            /G#m            /
    It's just a mistake  I won't have to face  don't give it a name,  don't give it a
    Yeah babe, I know it gets dark,   down by Luna Park but everybody else is squeezing out a

A            /B              /E              /              /
place   don't give it a chance, it's lucky in a way                     It
spark that happened in the heat, somewhere in the dark,    in the dark    The

A            /B              /E              /A              /
must have felt strange to find me inside you    I hadn't intended to stay    Did
doctor gets nervous completing the service  he's all rubber gloves and no head    Yes, he

A            /B              /C#m    A    /B              /
you want to keep it right, put it to sleep at night, squeeze it until it could say   you can't be too
fumbles the light switch, it's just another minor hitch, wishes to  God he was dead but you can't be too
```

CHORUS (see tab)..

```
C#m        A    /B              /C#m    A    /B              /
strong                You can't be too strong              You can't be too
................................  Pause...............
C#m        A    B   /E    E    /A              /E              /
strong                Can't be too strong              You decide what's
1st time only
Badd4            /E              /Aadd2          /E              /
wrong

Badd4            /              ://|
```

2nd time   GRADUAL FADE OUT

```
B            /E              /A              /E              /
wrong            Can't be too hard.          Too tough.        Too

B            /E              /A              /E              /
rough.      Too right too wrong  And you   can't be too strong.      Baby!

A            /E              / etc
```

YOU CAN'T BE TOO STRONG
(The 'add' chords)

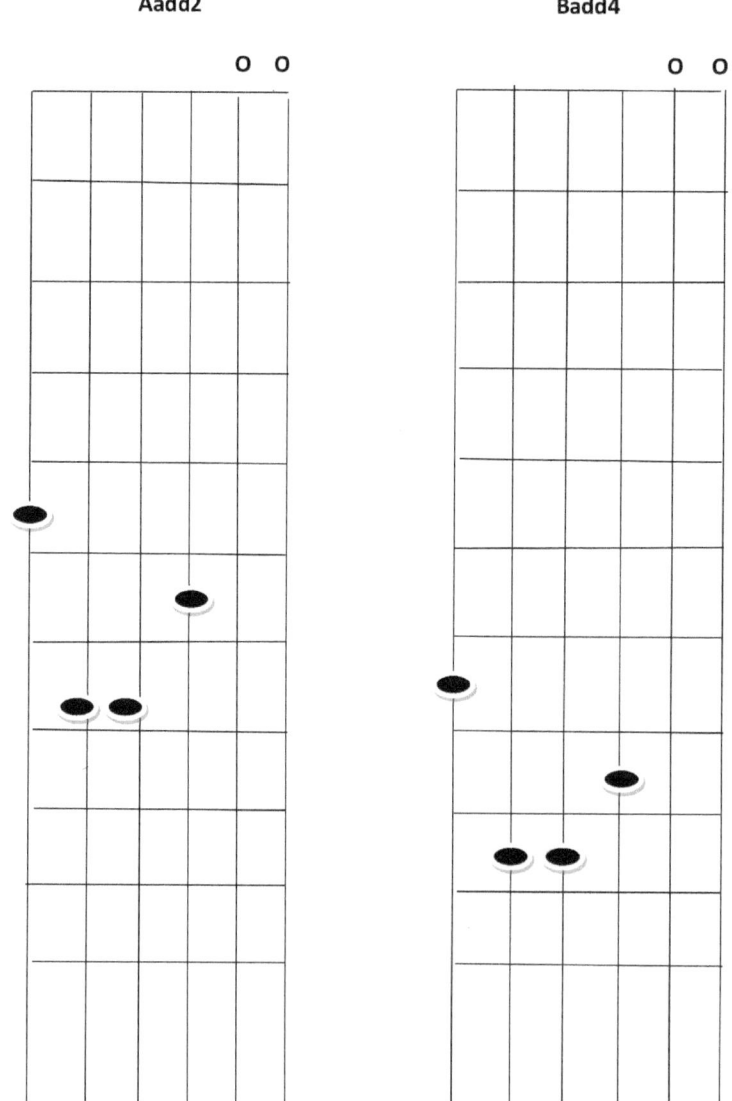

Aadd2   Badd4

YOU CAN'T BE TOO STRONG
ACOUSTIC RIFFS

YOU CAN'T BE TOO STRONG
ACOUSTIC RIFFS -

40

PASSION IS NO ORDINARY WORD

4/4

INTRO

F#m   /C#m   E A /D   /   /

VERSES 1 & 2

//:A   /E   A   /D   A   /
   It worked much better in a f a n t a s y   Imagination's one thing comes
   We got new idols for   the   screen to – day Although they make a lot of noises they got

E   /
easy to me
nothing to say

A   /E   A   /D   A   /
 'Cause this is nothing else if not un - real When I pretend to touch you, you pre-
  I try to look amazed but   it's an   act   the movie might be new but it's the

         Pause
E   E   (F bass)/
tend to feel
same soundtrack

CHORUS 1 (1st time only)

F#m   D   /E   /F#m   D   /E   /
Passion is no ordinary word,   passion is no ordinary   word
                    Push   Push   Push
F#m   D   /C#m   /D   /Bm   E   /
Passion is no ordinary word, ain't manufactured   or just another sound That you hear at

F#m   /C#m   E A /D   ://
night   at night

CHORUS 2

F#m   D   /E   /F#m   D   /E   /
Passion is no ordinary word,   passion is no ordinary   word
                    Push   Push   Push
F#m   D   /C#m   /D   /Bm   E   /
Passion is no ordinary word, ain't manufactured   or just another sound That you hear at
                   STOP 2   3   4
F#m   /F#m   D   D /
night

BRIDGE

```
E              /F#m          /E      A      /D        E        /
   Say how it feels    Real useless ain't it   Wait until it bites right down inside you

F#m         C#m       /D       E           /
   The world is easy when you're just playing around with it

F#m         E      /F#m      E     /F#m        E          /
Everything's a thrill   and every girl's a kill   And then it gets unreal    and

D          /E              /
then you don't feel anything
```

SOLO

```
F#m   D   /E        /F#m   D   /E       /F#m   D   /E           /
          You don't feel anything        You don't feel anything

                                         Push      Push
F#m   D   /E        /F#m   D   /C#m      /D               /D    /

D         /D        /
```

VERSE 3 (AS VERSES 1 & 2)

An object of desire you don't desire to be
Ah but the shop window dummies give in just as easily
I try to stop but have to make you drop down to the floor
Moaning in the darkness as we fake some more

CHORUS 3 & 4

```
F#m        D    /E          /F#m        D    /E            /
Passion is no ordinary word,     passion is no ordinary   word

                 Push             Push            Push    STOP
F#m        D    /C#m             /D              /Bm       EE  /
Passion is no ordinary word, ain't manufactured or just another sound  That you hearing

F#m        D    /E          /F#m        D    /E            /
Passion is no ordinary word,     passion is no ordinary   word

                 Push             Push            Push
F#m        D    /C#m             /D              /Bm       E   /
Passion is no ordinary word, ain't manufactured or just another sound  That you hear at
```

SLOW FADE..

```
F#m       /C#m   E  A /D        /D        /D       /D      /D etc
night      at night
```

42

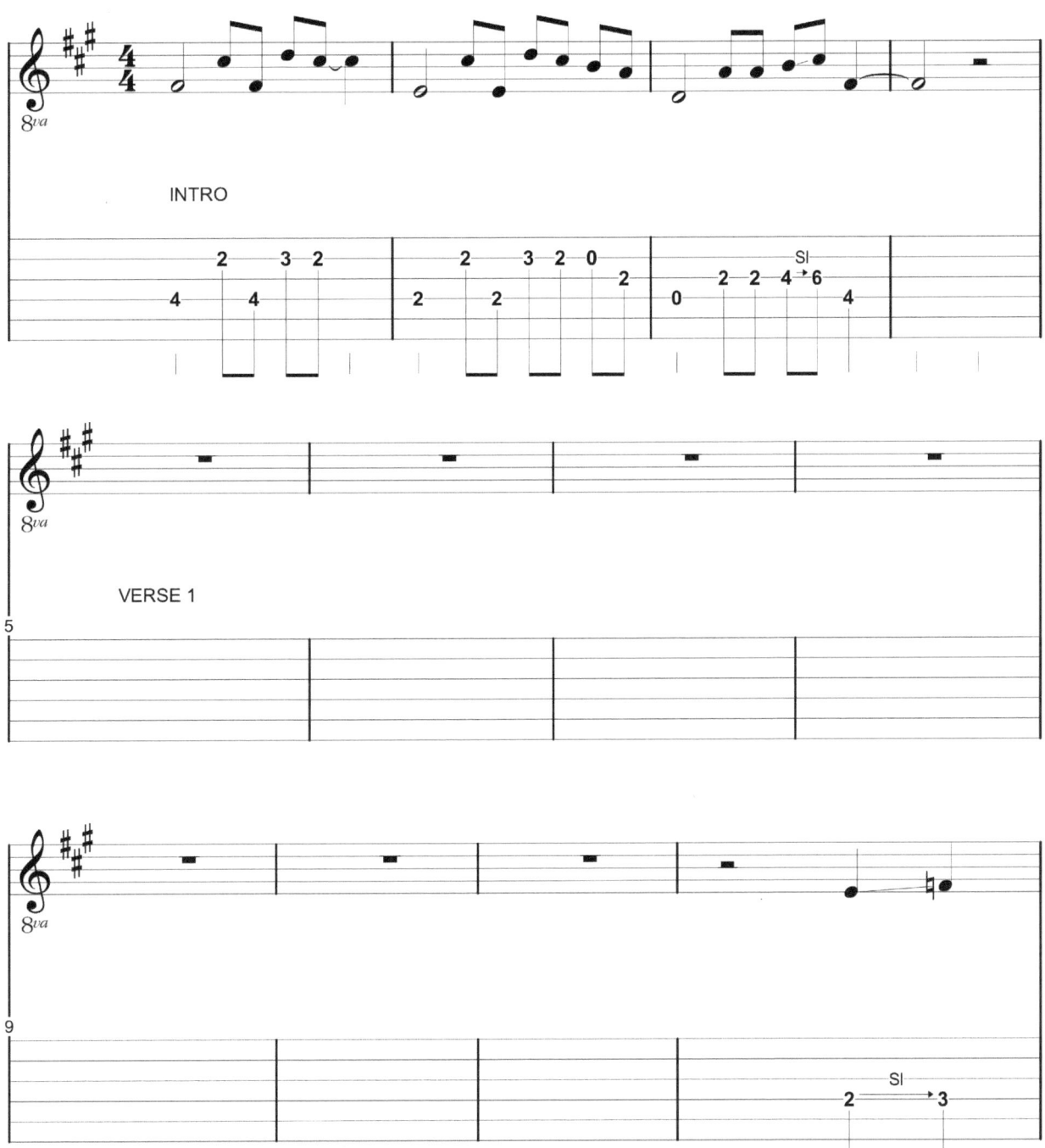

PASSION IS NO ORDINARY WORD
LEAD GUITAR -

44

PASSION IS NO ORDINARY WORD
LEAD GUITAR -

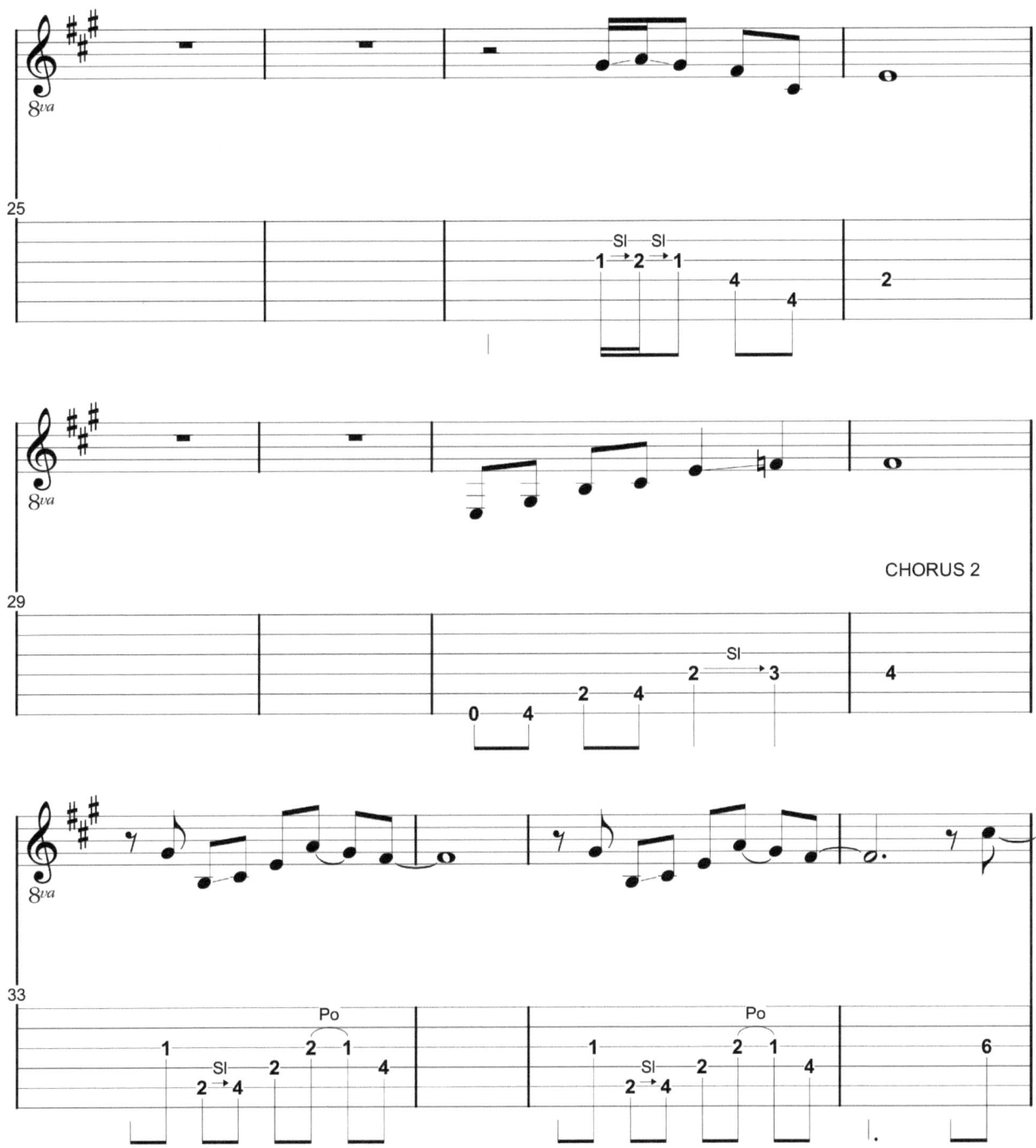

45

PASSION IS NO ORDINARY WORD
LEAD GUITAR -

BRIDGE

PASSION IS NO ORDINARY WORD
LEAD GUITAR -

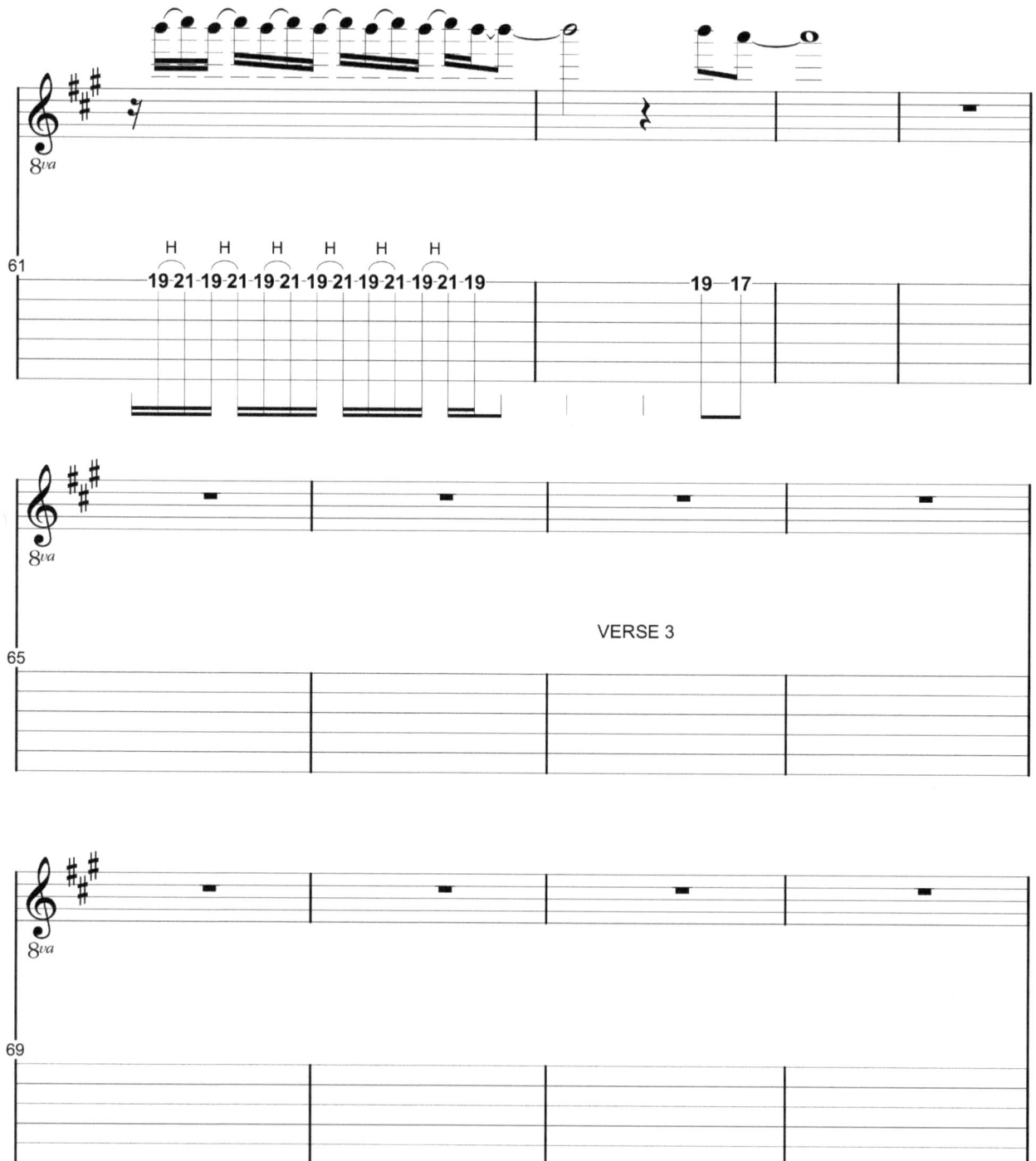

PASSION IS NO ORDINARY WORD
LEAD GUITAR -

PASSION IS NO ORDINARY WORD
LEAD GUITAR -

OUTRO

FADE OUT

PASSION IS NO ORDINARY WORD
LEAD GUITAR -

RECORDS

Graham Parker's tale of fear and drama

Squeezing Out Sparks
Graham Parker and
the Rumour
Arista

By Greil Marcus

GRAHAM PARKer's first two albums remain among the very finest of the decade: lyrical, intense, emotionally specific; a rough and untrained voice somehow merging perfectly with the Anglicized *Blonde on Blonde* /Stax-Volt classicism of the band. It was a signal debut, *Howlin Wind* and *Heat Treatment* both arriving in 1976 along with a string of Let's-Conquer-the-U.S.A. club dates. Then Parker and the Rumour had to deal with commercial success, or rather the lack of it: to find themselves an audience or else face a foreclosed future of second-on-the-bill, short-term contracts and premature breakup, their best music perhaps ahead of them and out of reach.

Things did not work out. English punk—which Parker had anticipated with his working-class fury, if not his style—appeared, and made him seem irrelevant, or, worse, tame. Elvis Costello (who, when I first heard him, sounded to me like a hoax that Parker and his sometime producer Nick Lowe had thought up in an inspired moment) emerged with music and an image that could at once take off from punk and escape its enemies. More obsessed, savvy and market-

Rolling Stone

June 28th, 1979 • Issue No. 294

Graham Parker: rumour becomes fact

By James Henke

CLEVELAND

BOB ANDREWS looks like a middle-aged minister who's gone off on a bender at a church social. Dressed in black pants, shirt and suit coat, the balding keyboard player for Graham Parker and the Rumour darts around the dance floor at the Agora Ballroom, jumping up and down, clapping and shouting at the singer up onstage.

It's Wednesday night—"ladies' night"—at the Agora, a showcase dance club located on a scurvy side street in the desolate downtown area near Cleveland State University. The previous evening, a packed house turned out to see Graham Parker and the Rumour, and now Parker and company are back, doing a special show that was announced over a local radio station only a few hours earlier. Unfortunately, because of the short notice, the group finds itself facing not another crowd of fanatics, as has been the case for much of this first leg of Parker's three-month U.S. tour, but a sparse, unattentive audience of a few hundred clean-cut college couples who no doubt showed up to hear a few brews and listen to cover versions of late-Sixties and early-Seventies hits performed by a local group called Lefty. And Andrews is trying his best to set an example for the crowd.

"Get that heckler out of here," Parker shouts, pointing toward the keyboard player. "He's been following me all over the country," Andrews continues his antics, and Parker bends down to take swigs from cans of Michelob and Miller offered up to him by the few faithful at the foot of the stage. "Why do they call Cleveland the rock & roll capital of the world?" Parker continues, a sneer crossing his face. "What the fuck do they mean by rock & roll — buzz-saw guitars or something? Well, don't worry, we'll be doing our Beatles medley in a minute."

Instead, the Rumour rips into a roaring version of "Soul Shoes." Andrews scurries back up behind his keyboards as Parker prowls the stage like a caged leopard, occasionally stopping at the edge to lift his large, tinted spectacles and peer into the eyes of the crowd. By the end of the song, Parker and the Rumour have stirred up enough enthusiasm that they are called back for an encore.

But it is still far from the victory Parker had hoped to win when he agreed to do the show for free. Backstage, Andrews begins talking about the couples who walked out during the performance. "It was the girls," he says. "Did you see them? The kind who sit at home and watch the detergent and fabric-softener adverts. The guys seemed to be getting into it, but their girlfriends *[Cont. on 23]*

Graham Parker

[Cont. from 9] were grabbing there: "Come on, Henry. We've got to get home and do the laundry."

Parker, slumped down on a love seat in the dressing room, is not in a jolting mood. "It's depressing," he moans. "It's so fucking depressing."

GRAHAM PARKER HAS been waging such battles against indifference for years. Born in 1950 in London, Parker grew up in Deepcut, a country village in southeast England. His mother worked in a cafe and his father was a coal stoker. Parker left school when he was seventeen and began working at the Animal Viral Research Institute, breeding mice and guinea pigs. But he soon found that job, like most other aspects of working-class life in England, a dead end.

His way of breaking through that was music. In 1975, after a series of odd jobs and stints in several bands, Parker, then a gas-station attendant, sent a tape of some songs he'd written to London's Hope and Anchor pub. Dave Robinson, who ran a recording studio there, heard the tape, got in touch with Parker and matched him up with the Rumour, an all-star band made up of veterans of England's then-waning pub-rock scene.

The following year, Parker and the Rumour — guitarists Brinsley Schwarz and Martin Belmont, keyboardist Andrews, bassist Andrew Bodnar and drummer Steve Goulding — released two albums. *Howlin Wind* and *Heat Treatment* contain some of the most intense music of the Seventies, showing off a variety of influences, from Bob Dylan and R&B to Van Morrison and reggae. With Parker's growling voice pulling everything together, it was clear that Graham Parker and the Rumour had risen above pub-rock to create their own distinct brand of rock & roll. As critic Greil Marcus put it: "Parker's advent was a sign that the decade was finally roughening up in its anger, its lyricism, its sophistication, its lack of artiness, its humor and its punch, his music cut a swath through most everything around it." But despite the critical acclaim, those first two LPs sold only 30,000 and 60,000 copies respectively.

The group and its management put much of the blame on Mercury Records, their label at the time. "Let's use *Howlin Wind* as an example," Allen Frey, Parker's U.S. representative, told me over dinner the night before the first Cleveland show. "We were out there touring in support of that album, which had such incredible reviews, and here Mercury had done an initial pressing of only 8000 copies. At that rate, you're lucky if there's even one copy in every city you play."

(A Mercury representative contends that although the company initially pressed 8000 copies, "substantially more records" were in the stores by the time of the tour.)

The third LP, *Stick to Me*, released late in 1977, was not as well received by the rock press, which criticized Nick Lowe's production, as well as some of Parker's songs. And the two-record live set that followed last year, *The Parkerilla*, was at best a flawed attempt to capture the band's powerful live presence on vinyl.

The day of the second Agora show, Parker defended *Stick to Me*. "I think it's very hard sounding, very English sounding," he said. "It's not meant to be played on an expensive hi-fi; I don't think it works then, perhaps." He added that the album had originally been recorded with producer Bob Potter, but that version was scrapped when they found it was impossible to mix. ("The hi-hat kept going over everything, and there was something missing in the bass frequencies"). The Nick Lowe version had to be recorded in a week, crammed in between tours of Sweden and the U.K.

Parker did admit that *The Parkerilla* was not as good as it should have been. But he maintained that this was not because he rushed it

> 'There wasn't enough care taken on "The Parkerilla." I wasn't experienced enough; I think we botched it.'

out just to fulfill his contract with Mercury — the reason most often cited in the press. "There wasn't enough care taken on *The Parkerilla*. I wasn't experienced enough, so I left it up to my manager and whoever he got to do the sound. And I think we botched it."

Despite his lack of commercial success, Parker had no trouble finding a new label. In fact, an intense round of bidding reportedly preceded his signing with Arista Records. His first album for the label, *Squeezing Out Sparks*, and the accompanying tour have gone a long way toward regaining the momentum that was lost after the first two LPs. The critical response has equaled, if not surpassed, that given Parker's first two records. And at press time, the LP was in the Top Forty with a bullet and had sold more than 200,000 copies.

In addition to being the first album for a new label, *Squeezing Out Sparks* also marks the beginning of a new musical era for Parker. The horns and complex

G.P. and the Rumour: Bodnar, Goulding, Andrews, Belmont, Parker, Schwarz

The Pazz & Jop Critics' Poll (Almost) Grows Up

By Robert Christgau

A few weeks ago two rock critics were gossiping on the phone, something rock critics do more than ever now that there aren't any press parties. Both were among the many newcomers asked to contribute to the sixth or seventh annual Pazz & Jop Critics' Poll, and both were awed by this responsibility, as is only mete. One of them, however, was apparently overawed, he—I assume it's a he, since most rock critics are—told my informant he felt like he'd been knighted. A jest, of course, but nevertheless—I mean, I'm obviously not the only one who takes this thing seriously. Every year I am beset by late ballots via special delivery and express mail; messengers and living critics come up to the fifth floor to hand me and my fellow Poobah their lists. And for what? No one is paid, and very few ballots are reprinted. As the poll gets larger the power of any individual to affect the result diminishes. But people actually listen again to dozens of albums, agonize, call long distance to clarify our chronically incomprehensible letter of invitation, all to assure that the tally reflects their deepest convictions. Ain't representative democracy grand?

Representative of what, you might ask, and I admit I could be happier with the answer. This was to be the year the P&JCP grew up; I vowed that in 1979 I'd start tackling the problems of regional and racial spread early. But that vow, like others before it, went down to defeat. Instead I spent two days in mid-December working phones with co-Poobah Tom Carson. Our method was simple—frantic calls to acquaintances all over the country to ascertain who was actually reviewing records where, never mind how well—and its effectiveness scattershot. We did better in Minneapolis than Chicago and lousy indeed through the southeastern and Rocky Mountain states. It doesn't bother me that L.A. and Boston are disproportionately represented, or that New York provided 66 of the 155 critics who responded. Those are the cities where the outlets are, and anyway, this is still a *Voice* poll—all Riffs contributors who hear a lot of records are included in automatically. But nobody from Nashville or Denver or Omaha or New Orleans was even invited, and this is a good time to mention that any regularly published rock critic with access to most of the important releases who'd like to be in should write now and I'll file his or her address. Go knight yourself.

Racial balance proved even more difficult to come by. Our informants were useless, and consultation with black journalists around here yielded few new names. Finally, around New Year's, I resorted to record company publicists specializing in black music, but most of the 30 or so invitations that resulted went out so late that I got only 11 back in time, enough to suss certain patterns but not enough to see them fully realized in the tally. The post office was a big problem in general. A lot of people got our instructions 10 or 12 days after they were mailed, or never, and when no first-class letters were delivered to the paper on deadline day we were forced to postpone the final count for 24 hours. Even so, late ballots kept dribbling in afterwards, including several from black critics and several others from regional punkzines, which were also contacted late. Next year we've got to get organized.

As it was, though, I think the poll ended up pretty much what it should have been in a very enjoyable but critically inconclusive year. Four "r&b" acts (the term is returning to favor) made the album list, expanded this year from 30 to 40 in honor of an enlarged electorate and the curly-headed kid in the third row. More black input would have meant more commanding finishes for all four—crossover queen Donna Summer, comeback prince Michael Jackson, disco pacemakers Chic, and elder statesman Stevie Wonder—as well as for Ashford & Simpson (*Stay Free*, 44th), probably Dionne Warwick (*Dionne*,

The winner: Graham Parker & The Rumour's "Squeezing Out Sparks"

1979 Pazz & Jop Critics' Poll: Albums

1.	Graham Parker & The Rumour: *Squeezing Out Sparks* (Arista)	767 (63)
2.	Neil Young & Crazy Horse: *Rust Never Sleeps* (Reprise)	652 (50)
3.	The Clash (Epic)	638 (50)
4.	Talking Heads: *Fear of Music* (Sire)	620 (51)
5.	Elvis Costello: *Armed Forces* (Columbia)	619 (55)
6.	Van Morrison: *Into the Music* (Warner Bros.)	474 (41)
7.	The B-52s (Warner Bros.)	371 (37)
8.	Tom Petty and the Heartbreakers: *Damn the Torpedoes* (Backstreet/MCA)	340 (31)
9.	Pere Ubu: *Dub Housing* (Chrysalis)	334 (28)
10.	Donna Summer: *"Bad Girls"* (Casablanca)	330 (30)
11.	The Roches (Warner Bros.)	292 (30)
12.	Dave Edmunds: *Repeat When Necessary* (Swan Song)	222 (21)
13.	Nick Lowe: *Labour of Lust* (Columbia)	201 (24)
14.	Tom Verlaine (Elektra)	192 (22)
15.	Iggy Pop: *New Values* (Arista)	190 (20)
16.	Marianne Faithfull: *Broken English* (Island)	185 (20)
17.	Blondie: *Eat to the Beat* (Chrysalis)	184 (20)
18.	Michael Jackson: *Off the Wall* (Epic)	179 (16)
19.	Rickie Lee Jones (Warner Bros.)	176 (20)
20.	Buzzcocks: *Singles Going Steady* (I.R.S.)	172 (18)
21.	Fleetwood Mac: *Tusk* (Warner Bros.)	160 (17)
22.	Neil Young & Crazy Horse: *Live Rust* (Reprise)	158 (15)
23.	Ry Cooder: *Bop Till You Drop* (Warner Bros.)	155 (18)
24.	David Johansen: *In Style* (Blue Sky)	136 (15)
25.	Lene Lovich: *Stateless* (Stiff/Epic)	125 (13)
26.	Linton Kwesi Johnson: *Forces of Victory* (Mango)	122 (13)
27.	Chic: *Risqué* (Atlantic)	112 (11)
28.	Joe Jackson: *Look Sharp!* (A&M)	111 (11)
29.	Art Ensemble of Chicago: *Nice Guys* (ECM)	108 (10)
30.	Roxy Music: *Manifesto* (Atlantic)	107 (11)
31.	David Bowie: *Lodger* (RCA Victor)	104 (12)
32.	The Slits: *Cut* (Antilles)	99 (10)
33.	Philip Glass/Robert Wilson: *Einstein on the Beach* (Tomato)	98 (9)
34.	Bob Marley & The Wailers: *Survival* (Island)	94 (9)
35.	The Police: *Reggatta de Blanc* (A&M)	92 (10)
36.	Shoes: *Present Tense* (Elektra)	90 (12)
37.	The Jam: *All Mod Cons* (Polydor)	89 (9)
38.	Bob Dylan: *Slow Train Coming* (Columbia)	88 (11)
39.	Stevie Wonder's *Journey Through the Secret Life of Plants* (Tamla)	88 (9)
40.	The Kinks: *Low Budget* (Arista)	85 (9)

52nd), and possibly Millie Jackson (*Live and Uncensored*, 55th). More punkzine input would have helped the *nouvelle vague concrete* of Pere Ubu, the reggae agitprop of Linton Kwesi Johnson, the maximal minimalism of Philip Glass, and the elderly statesmanship of Iggy Pop, as well as pushing *Off White* (45th) and/or *Buy the Contortions* (47th)—James Chance's two albums, which totaled 139 points on a spottily distributed independent label—into the top 40, and perhaps aiding XTC (*Drums and Wires*, 49th) and Wire (*154*, 53rd) as well. Both constituencies would have boosted Bob Marley, and either might have gone for the jazz records that got scattered mention: not only the Art Ensemble's *Nice Guys*, but also *Mingus at Antibes* (48th)—three Mingus albums totaled 121 points— *Air Lore* (51st), and Blood Ulmer's (excuse me, I mean James Blood's) *Tales of Captain Black* (60th). And they would have upped the disco discs and imports on the singles chart.

But especially if allowances are made for Nashville and Denver and Omaha and New Orleans, it's hard to imagine any other album cracking this year's top five: *Armed Forces*, by last year's overpowering winner, Elvis Costello; *Fear of Music*, by Talking Heads, up from fifth in 1978; the confusing American version of *The Clash*, which in its 1977 English edition showed up on a lot of best-of-the-decade lists; *Rust Never Sleeps*, generally regarded as Neil Young's best album since *Tonight's the Night*; and this year's model, *Squeezing Out Sparks*, by Graham Parker & the Rumour, who placed their first two albums at two and four in the 1976 poll but haven't made much noise among the voters since.

The 1978 P & JCP's consensus was, in the immortal words of my editor, a "triumph of the new wave," with 16 of the top 30 albums falling clearly into the category and lots of others on the fringe despite increased participation by suspected conservatives. Not that I considered the triumph unmixed—my punkophile elation was undercut by my natural distrust of hegemony, especially defensive hegemony based on ressentiment. Commercially, after all, *Saturday Night Fever* and its trentuple platinum was spearheading its own victorious vanguard, and I detected in the sweep some of the racism and homophobia of "disco sucks," then a mere slogan rather than an arrogantly out-of-it prefab "movement." But it did seem that new wave was over the bottom line—that the best artists in the style (or whatever it is and was) were going to make albums for quite a while—and that print media were part of its success. It had always been a truism of the record manufacturers (and of music journalists) that good reviews don't sell enough product to keep anybody but the reviewers in business. But recently it's become apparent that between the prestige they impart and the core audience they generate (especially in the absence of adventurous radio), good reviews do keep good bands, in the immortal words of the Bee Gees, "stayin' alive."

That was last year. Since then, an arrogantly out-of-it prefab industry has taken a nasty fall, with some blame due both trentuple platinum (and the consequent lure of overproduction) and disco (now regarded once again as a cult music with crossover potential). As a consequence, there are rock and roll propagandists who'll tell you that new wave's triumph isn't just artistic—that last year's critical consensus is next year's big thing. As usual, I don't believe it'll happen, and furthermore I don't want anyone else to. I'm delighted that Blondie's *Parallel Lines*, which finished 25th in the 1978 P&JCP, subsequently achieved the AM airplay and platinum sales its inspired popcraft deserved, and pleased enough

Continued on next page

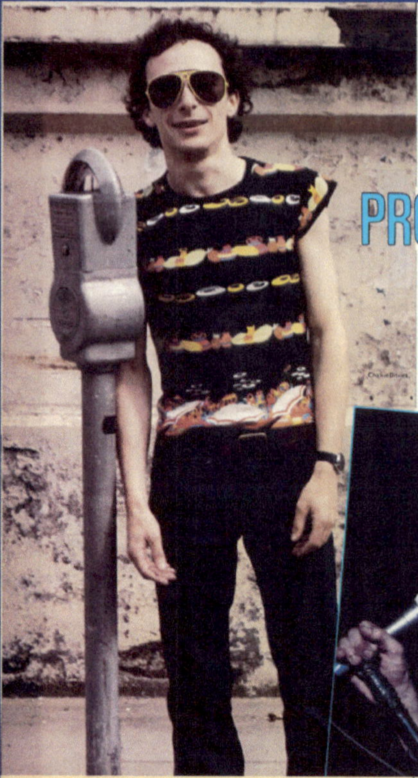

GRAHAM PARKER SEEKS PROTECTION

by Susan Whitall

It was Toronto, a soft late May evening, and the Best Promo Girl in Detroit and I were watching Graham Parker and the Rumour fight a losing battle with the El Mocambo Club's sound system. They were able to blast out a handful of songs in between power blackouts, one of which,

(Left) 'Scuse me—can I park here?
(Right) Biting the mike that feeds him.

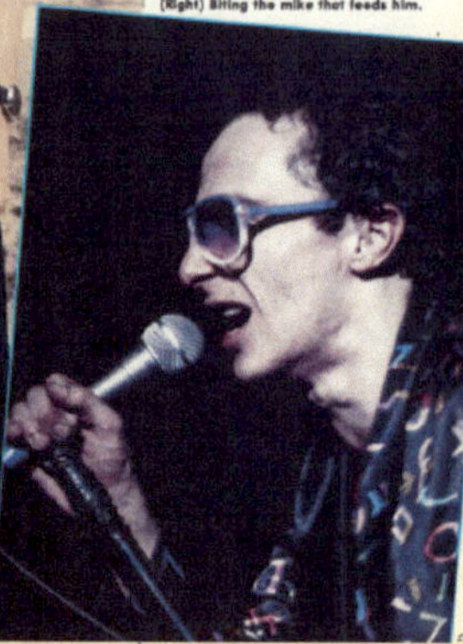

now is the re-creation of the Mod. The two Who movies, *The Kids Are Alright* and *Quadrophenia*, arguably, started it off. And for a short time there was a vogue of young bands re-creating Who moves on stage that had record company and press people asking "Is *this* the Big New Thing?" But no, the true Mod revival is Mod-ska—the bluebeat that pre-dated reggae. The Who were *the* Mod-pop band, ska was *the* Mod dance beat. And so it is in revival, with Elvis Costello producing the highly acclaimed debut album from ska-revival band The Specials. Parker also finds it pretty hard not to identify with the '79 version of the Mod; after all, he went through the original number when Prince Buster invented the genre back in '67. His t-shirt just about sums it up. "Fuck Art," it's emblazoned, "Let's Dance."

"It's a bit surprising to me, though, that all these kids have got into it [ska]. I mean, I don't know how it's happened. You know, I wish they'd think up their own new fashion sometimes. I mean, it's quite fun for them, I suppose, innit? Ska was good for me because, when I became a hippie (when I was about 18, 19), I was a bit more cynical than most of the people around me. They seemed like they could get dragged into anything—Jesus or what have you—and I could sit back a bit, because I'd been through this Mod thing which made me a bit tough. Y'know, you were one of the boys and stuff. So things don't go to my head as much as they did to some people. That gave me a good background in some ways..."

Back to the new wave. In retrospect, do you think you predated the genre?

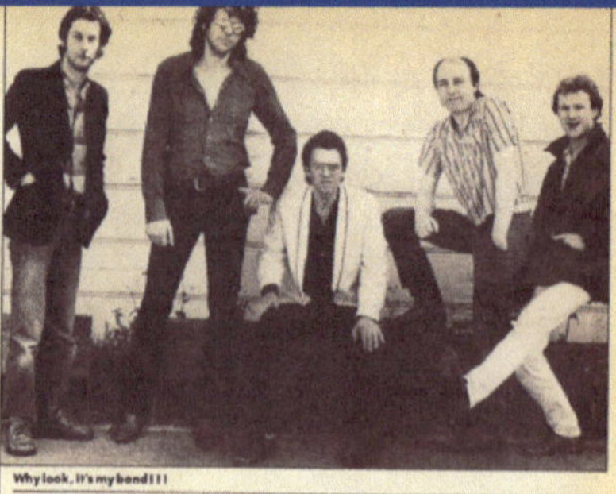

Why look, it's my band!!!

"I'd like the record company to be involved, but you get so many wankers whose opinion

around for *Heat Treatment*. So it's like, a lot of energy is expended on a first album, which is unrepeatable, really. People may have seen that in *Howlin' Wind*."

How "easy" had it been then, to get things organized for Howlin' Wind?

"Well, the reason I was doing jobs like selling gas was because it was *undemanding*, and I was only doing it in the morning, and afternoons I could write or sit around and get stoned. Or try and find musicians

Graham laughed, "used to sing those Jamaican words, and I didn't even know what I was singing, I was copying the sounds! [*Breaks into song*]: Amalutta lutta shanty town... Sort of...kids, you know? It was good fun..."

Then, later...

"Uh, I've traveled around the world, you know." (This provoked laughter, for some reason...I dunno, the tape has a life of its own.)

"Gibraltar and Guernsey...France, Spain. You know, traveled around with an acoustic, rippin' off James Taylor and Donovan, and doin' that kind of stuff." Disbelieving laughter.

"Oh, *yeah*! I used to finger-pick...that was like '72, '73, I was doin' all that solo singer/songwriter stuff—just completely amateur. People who heard me used to like it—I used to write loads of songs, hundreds and hundreds, but they were all kind of—you know, post-LSD experience songs."

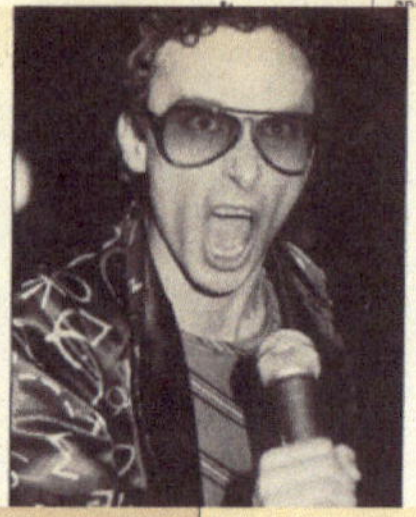

Rainbow—in a hamburger cafe, and he'd play slide guitar with me, and people'd be eating and they'd listen—and that's what I was doin'. I was learnin' to sing, then. Before that I used to play at parties around my home area, I mean, I'd been in loads of groups! But nothing professional—when I was fifteen, youth clubs and just stuff like that...no name, *nothing*. But I only really learned to sing when I went through this thing singing in this cafe, and sittin' up in Dave Robinson's studio 'til two in the morning, singing everything I'd written to him, and taping it. I started to learn to sing, and get better. So I was pretty much an amateur...

"When I first went onstage with a band, it was a big deal—I was really scared, it was the first real thing I'd done where I knew my name would end up in the *Melody Maker*!

"You know, the first gig, I thought, my whole life was *here*, at the Nag's Head in

GRAHAM PARKER: Discovering Élan

Hmmm, wonder who's on *Celebrity Sweepstakes* tonight...

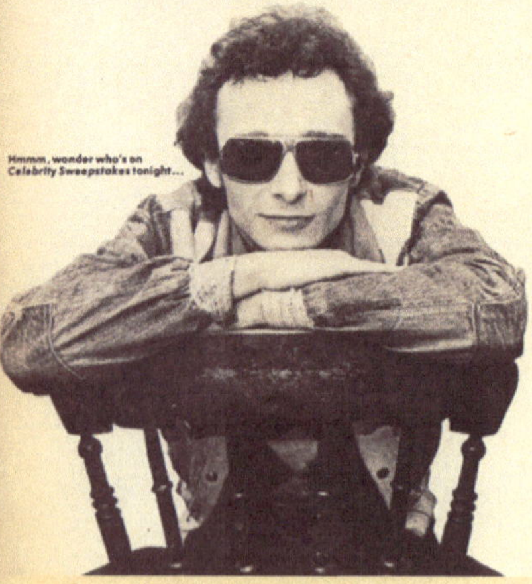

by Nigel Burnham

LONDON—Graham Parker's now 28, he's barely begun his career in rock (less than four years ago, he was serving in a gas station), and he's already been called "one of the decade's great white R&B artists." In recent months, nevertheless, much has been made of the fact that Parker has still not achieved the kind of record sales critics expect of a man of his caliber/reputation; much has also been made of Parker's return on *Squeezing Out Sparks* to the horn-less simplicity of *Howlin' Wind*. After his Australian tour, changes (it is predicted) are inevitable in the Parker camp's policy.

By now, however, Geep is plowing through his month-long Antipodean tour, and, recollecting the fervor with which his first one was received, he's looking forward to it.

☆☆☆

Why are you going to Australia and New Zealand, and to nowhere else? Wouldn't it be more logical to do it as part of a world tour, or at least to throw in Japan?

"Well, we were going to go to Japan, but seeing as it's our last record for Phonogram in Japan, the promoter phoned up about three weeks before the tour was arranged, and said, 'Look, Phonogram aren't helping us at all, we ain't gonna fill the gigs out'. So we just thought, there's just no point going with Phonogram back in there. Because they don't give a shit. It's just not worth taking a whole group to Japan if they're not going to fill out the places. Because, we did well last time, and we don't want to go back and do *worse*, y'know?"

How about your U.K. company? I guess the song "Mercury Poisoning" just about sums how you felt about the Mercury record company in America.

"Yeah, it's pretty much the same thing really. But you don't blame Mercury in the end. It's Polygram, which is based in Holland. And that's all Phonogram as well. I mean, they're not as bad as Mercury, but when it comes down to it they've got the same attitude. You know 'If you're lucky, it'll make it, if you're not, you don't work hard enough for it'. And the contract was up, and they expected me to sign again. And when we didn't, they really didn't get behind *Squeezing Out Sparks* in England at all, Phonogram. Real dumper..."

The conversation temporarily switches to Parker's increasing renown as (near enough) the premier songwriter of the age. CBS' new wonderkid, Ellen Foley, and The Pointer Sisters, have both recently acknowledged him through their covers of, respectively, "Thunder and Rain" and "Turned Up Too Late," and Parker rates them both—especially the latter interpretation.

"I think the whole album by The Pointers is great. But it's just very hard for the public

WAX

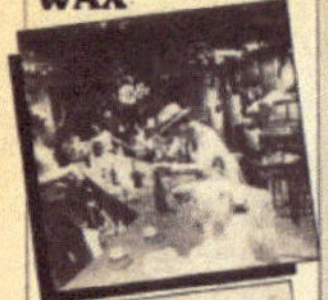

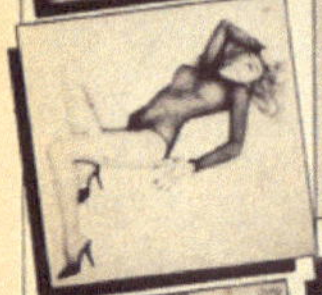

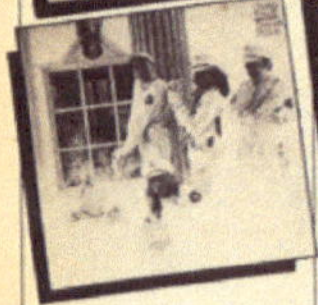

THE WINNERS!

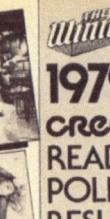

1979 CREEM READERS' POLL RESULTS

BEST R & B SINGLE
1. **Bad Girls (Donna Summer)**
2. You Gotta Serve Somebody (Bob Dylan)
3. Sail On (Commodores)
4. Hot Stuff (Donna Summer)
5. Boom, Boom (Pat Travers)
6. After The Love Is Gone (Earth, Wind & Fire)
7. Still (Commodores)
8. Pop Muzik (M)
9. Move It On Over (George Thorogood & the Destroyers)
10. I Will Survive (Gloria Gaynor)

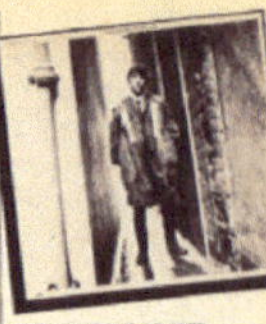

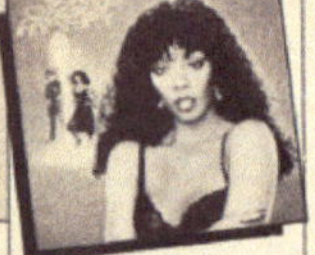

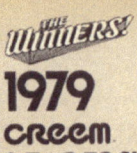

BEST R & B ALBUM
1. **Bad Girls (Donna Summer)**
2. The Jukes (Southside Johnny & the Asbury Jukes)
3. I Am (Earth, Wind & Fire)
4. Slow Train Coming (Bob Dylan)
5. Boogie Motel (Foghat)
6. In Through The Out Door (Led Zeppelin)
7. Move It On Over (George Thorogood & the Destroyers)
8. Rickie Lee Jones
9. Squeezing Out Sparks (Graham Parker & the Rumour)
10. Midnight Magic (Commodores)

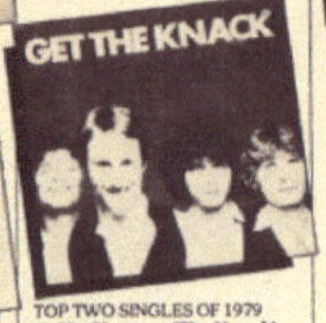

TOP TWO SINGLES OF 1979
1. **My Sharona (The Knack)**
2. **Let's Go (The Cars)**
3. Cruel To Be Kind (Nick Lowe)
4. I Want You To Want Me (Cheap Trick)
5. I Don't Like Mondays (Boomtown Rats)
6. Dream Police (Cheap Trick)
7. Pop Muzik (M)
8. I Was Made For Lovin' You (Kiss)
9. Long Live Rock (The Who)
10. Rock 'n' Roll Fantasy (Bad Co.)
11. My My Hey Hey (Neil Young)
12. I Fought The Law (The Clash)
13. Roxanne (The Police)
14. Superman (The Kinks)
15. Rock Lobster (B-52's)

TOP THREE ALBUMS OF 1979
1. **In Through The Out Door (Led Zeppelin)**
2. **Candy-O (The Cars)**
3. **Dream Police (Cheap Trick)**
4. Live At Budokan (Cheap Trick)
5. Rust Never Sleeps (Neil Young & Crazy Horse)
6. Squeezing Out Sparks (Graham Parker & the Rumour)
7. The Kids Are Alright (The Who)
8. Van Halen II (Van Halen)
9. Low Budget (The Kinks)
10. Get The Knack (The Knack)
11. The Clash
12. Dynasty (Kiss)
13. Fear Of Music (Talking Heads)
14. Armed Forces (Elvis Costello)
15. Labour Of Lust (Nick Lowe)
16. Highway To Hell (AC/DC)
17. B-52's
18. Breakfast In America (Supertramp)
19. Night In The Ruts (Aerosmith)
20. Look Sharp! (Joe Jackson)
21. Eat To The Beat (Blondie)
22. The Long Run (The Eagles)
23. Tusk (Fleetwood Mac)
24. Damn The Torpedoes (Tom Petty & the Heartbreakers)
25. You're Never Alone With A Schizophrenic (Ian Hunter)

BEST JAZZ ALBUM OF 1979
1. **A Taste For Passion (Jean-Luc Ponty)**
2. Chicago XIII
3. Mingus (Joni Mitchell)
4. Rise (Herb Alpert)
5. Morning Dance (Spyro Gyra)
6. I Want To Play For You (Stanley Clarke)
7. Live At The Hollywood Bowl (Chuck Mangione)
8. Rickie Lee Jones
9. Livin' Inside Your Love (George Benson)
10. 8:30 (Weather Report)

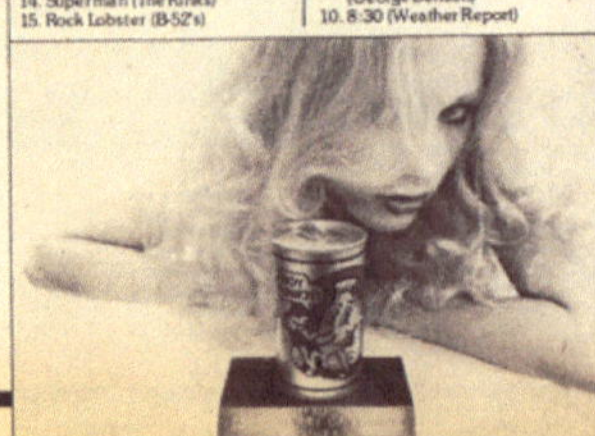

BEST REISSUE OF 1979
1. **Quadrophenia (The Who)**
2. The Kids Are Alright (The Who)
3. The Clash
4. The Essential Jimi Hendrix, Vol. II
5. "I Fought The Law" (The Clash)
6. "You're No Good" (Van Halen)
7. Greatest Hits (Rod Stewart)
8. "Ain't That A Shame" (Cheap Trick)
9. Shades Of Ian Hunter
10. "Money (Flying Lizards)

HOW WILL YOU FACE THE 80's?

"If the Beatles get back together, I'll throw up."
Lori A. Nielsen
Sterling Heights, MI

BEST NEW WAVE SINGLE
1. **Dreaming (Blondie)**
2. Rock Lobster (B-52's)
3. I Don't Like Mondays (Boomtown Rats)
4. Roxanne (The Police)
5. I Fought The Law (The Clash)
6. One Way Or Another (Blondie)
7. Message In A Bottle (The Police)
8. Is She Really Going Out With Him? (Joe Jackson)
9. Cruel To Be Kind (Nick Lowe)
10. Heart Of Glass (Blondie)

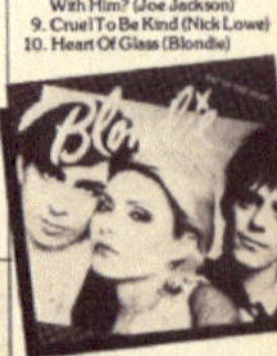

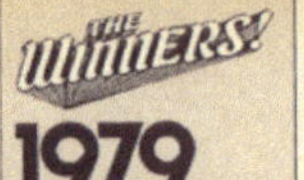

BEST NEW WAVE ALBUM
1. **Eat To The Beat (Blondie)**
2. The Clash
3. Fear Of Music (Talking Heads)
4. B-52's
5. Look Sharp! (Joe Jackson)
6. Duty Now For The Future (Devo)
7. Armed Forces (Elvis Costello)
8. Labour Of Lust (Nick Lowe)
9. Give 'Em Enough Rope (Clash)
10. Outlandos D'Amour (Police)

MARCH 1980

Woodward Studio's 29

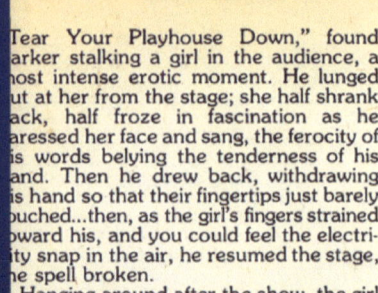

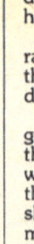

Tear Your Playhouse Down," found arker stalking a girl in the audience, a ost intense erotic moment. He lunged ut at her from the stage; she half shrank ack, half froze in fascination as he aressed her face and sang, the ferocity of is words belying the tenderness of his and. Then he drew back, withdrawing is hand so that their fingertips just barely ouched...then, as the girl's fingers strained oward his, and you could feel the electricity snap in the air, he resumed the stage, e spell broken.

Hanging around after the show, the girl as no longer the mysterious she Parker as squeezing sparks off of; she was just a

don't know how to move to the beat—they haven't got it.

"But they're gettin' off a bit...'cause we ram it down their throats. But basically they don't know what the fuck we're doing."

They're the flipside, emotionally, of the gutsy, sweaty type of crowds who swarm the clubs of these mid-continental cities when someone like G.P. & the R. *headline*, these sopered-out clone rock devotees. I shudder to say it, but it appears to be the midwestern younger generation *in toto*.

On the other hand, stalking the tough side streets of Toronto earlier with Promo Girl for food, when we saw an old man

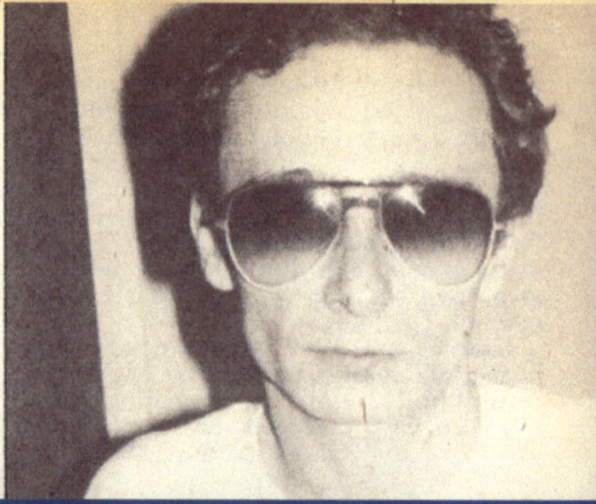

Graham Parker & Rick Nielsen explain their divide & conquer strategy for nubile taxidermy.

Top: from Creem magazine, 1979

Bottom: Graham Parker at the Park West, Chicago 1979

Upper left: Postcard promo 1979
Upper right: Graham Parker, Park West, Chicago 1979
Bottom: Brinsley Schwarz, Park West, Chicago 1979

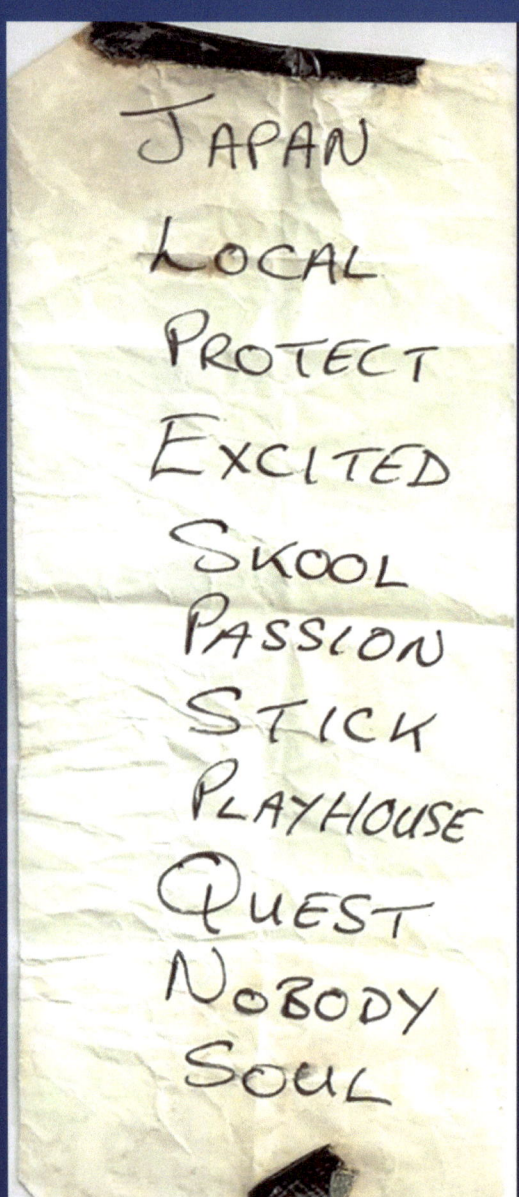

Setlist from:
Public Hall, Cleveland, OH
Friday 6/1/79

Autograph from:
Public Hall, Cleveland, OH
Friday 6/1/79

Ticket stub from:
The Shubert Theater, Philadelphia, PA
Tuesday 6/5/79

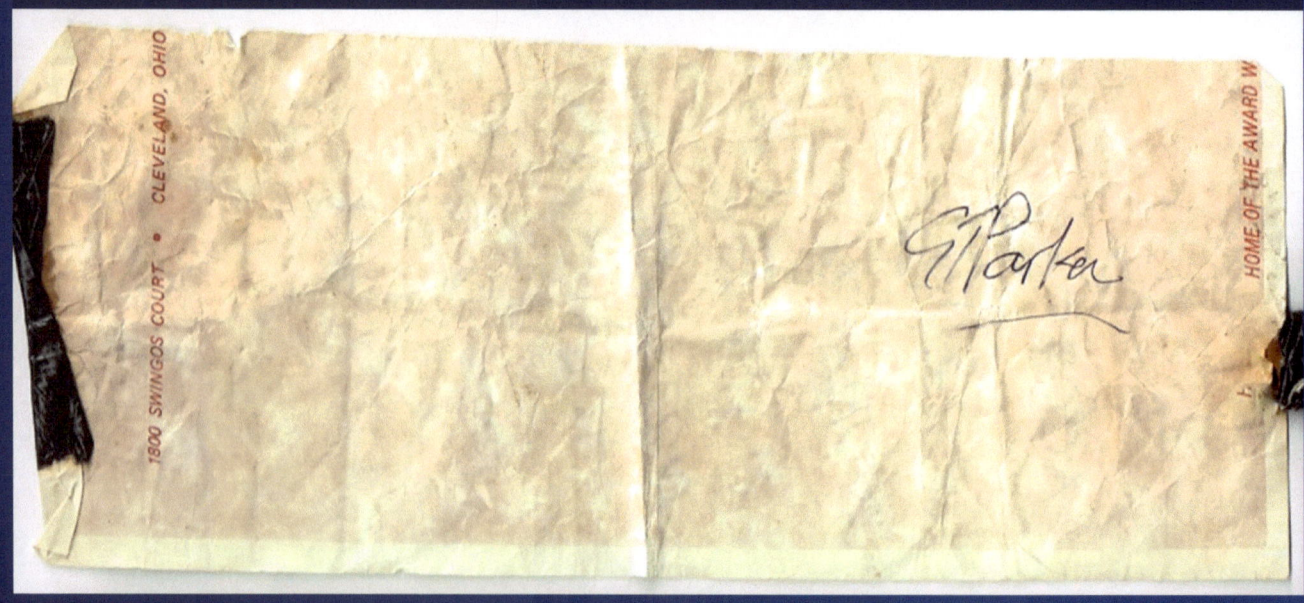

From the tour bus after the last gig at the Santa Monica Civic, 1979

More from the tour bus, 1979

" I have to do this. "

SATURDAY NITE IS DEAD
4/4

INTRO RIFF
```
     >                      >
D  Dsus   /D  Dm D /D   Dsus   /D  Dm D /
     >                      >
D  Dsus   /D  Dm D /D   Dsus   /D  Dm D /
```

VERSES 1 & 2

```
//:A              /Bm         /A           /D            /
```
Everybody just looks ugly now information don't compute
The ultraviolet light hurts me so it used to be my   friend

```
   A              /Bm         /D           /A            /
```
I draw a blank every time I think the football crowd has got the deadly boot   and
I once knew a good place to go   but now it's nowhere   like it was then   and

CHORUS 1st time only

```
D               /       /A        /D          /
```
Saturday nite is dead   Saturday nite is dead   It
STOP

```
Bm              /       /A        /          /
```
don't matter what they said you've got to use your own head   some day

```
D               /       /A        /Bm    E    /
```
Saturday nite is dead   Saturday nite is d e...a....d

INTRO RIFF 1st time only

```
D  Dsus   /D  Dm D /D   Dsus   /D  Dm D /D   Dsus   /D  Dm D :://
              Yeah its dead
```

CHORUS 2nd time

```
D               /       /A        /D          /
```
Saturday nite is dead   Saturday nite is dead   It
STOP

```
Bm              /       /A        /          /
```
don't matter what they said I'm going to the funeral Sunday

```
D               /       /A        /Bm    E    /
```
Saturday nite is dead   Saturday nite is d e...a...d

RIFF TO BRIDGE

```
     >        >        >        >
D  Dsus   /D  Dm   /A  Asus  /A  Am   /
Dead                              It
```

BRIDGE

```
C           F     /C   F     /C   F      /C    F       /
  must have been murder it ain't no accident   Oh no it means   nothing to me when the
PAUSE……………………………….
C              /              /
clock goes tick tick tick in my head

D              /              /              /              /
Saturday's dead               Saturday's dead
```

SOLO

```
//:E           /           /           /           ://
```

VERSE 3

```
A              /Bm           /A           /D           /
I look inside to find a place to hide but there ain't no place I know

              Pause…………………………..
A              /Bm           /           /
It's just as well that I'm stupefied

                                                    2/4
A              /G           /           /           /           /
it makes it easy   It makes it easy           to deliver  the fatal
4/4  >              >              >
D  Dsus   /D  Dm D /D  Dsus  /D  Dm D / D  Dsus  /D  Dm D /
blow              Deliver              Deliver              De-
     >
D  Dsus   /D  Dm D  /
liver              And
```

CHORUS 3

```
D              /              /A           /D           /
Saturday nite is dead         Saturday nite  is  dead         It
                                                        STOP
Bm             /              /A           /           /
don't matter what they said you got to use your own head  some day

D              /              /A           /Bm   E   /Bm   E   /
Saturday nite is dead         Saturday nite is d  e….a…d     D….e…..a…..d
```

OUTRO

D	Dsus	/D	Dm D	/D	Dsus	/D	Dm D	/ D	Dsus	/D	Dm D /
			Yeah It's dead						Saturday nite is dead		

D　Dsus　/D　Dm D　/ D　Dsus　/D　Dm D　/ D　Dsus　/D　Dm D /
Saturday nite is dead　　　Saturday nite is dead　　　Saturday nite is dead

D　Dsus　/D　Dm D　/ D　Dsus　/D　Dm D　/ D　Dsus　/D　Dm D /
Saturday nite is dead　　　Saturday nite is dead　　　Saturday nite is dead

D　Dsus　/D　Dm D　/ D　Dsus　/D　Dm D　/D　Dsus　/G
Saturday nite is dead　　　Saturday nite is dead　　　Saturday nite is dead

SATURDAY NITE IS DEAD
LEAD GUITAR

SATURDAY NITE IS DEAD
LEAD GUITAR -

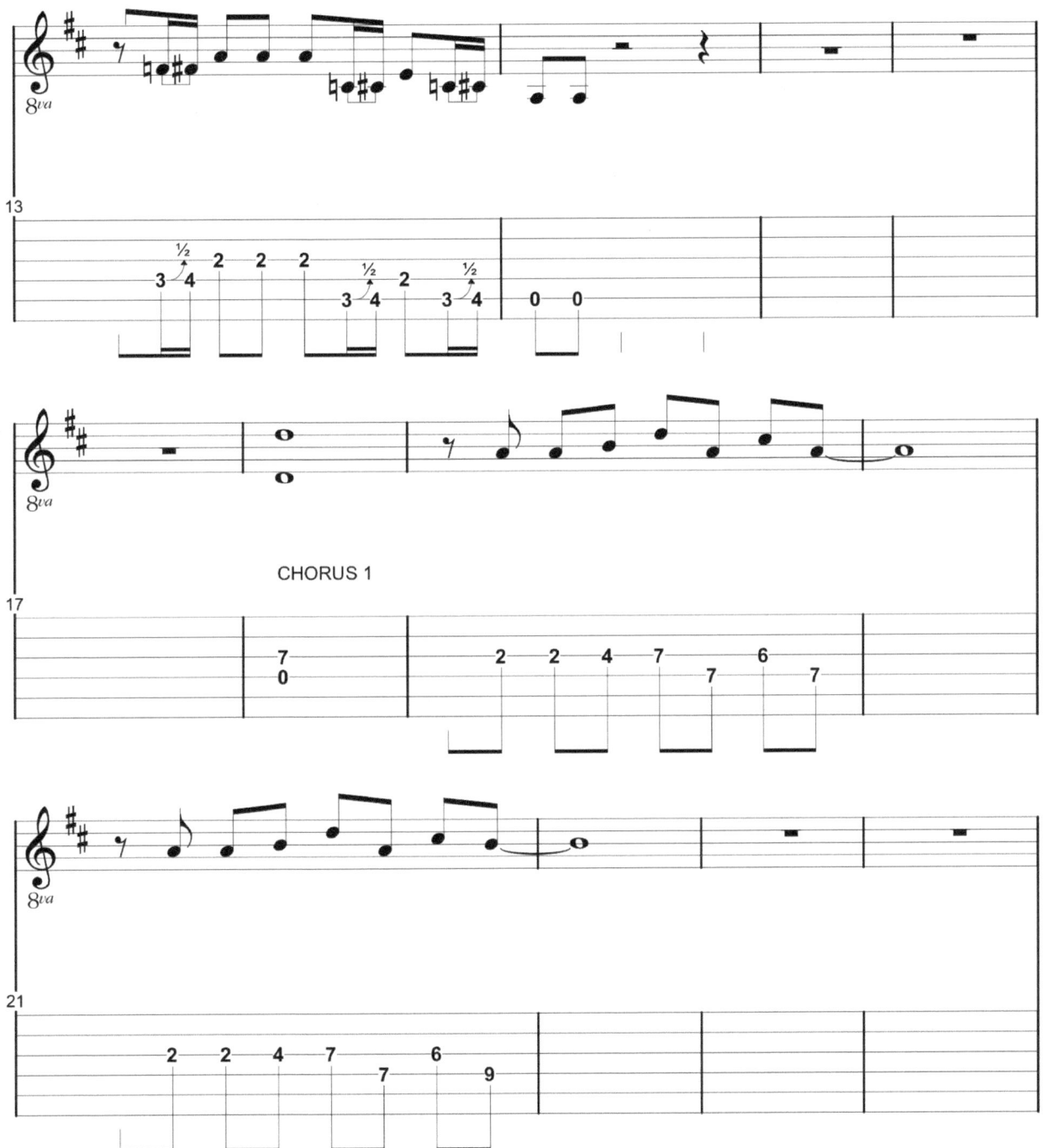

CHORUS 1

67

SATURDAY NITE IS DEAD
LEAD GUITAR -

SATURDAY NITE IS DEAD
LEAD GUITAR -

SATURDAY NITE IS DEAD
LEAD GUITAR -

SATURDAY NITE IS DEAD
LEAD GUITAR -

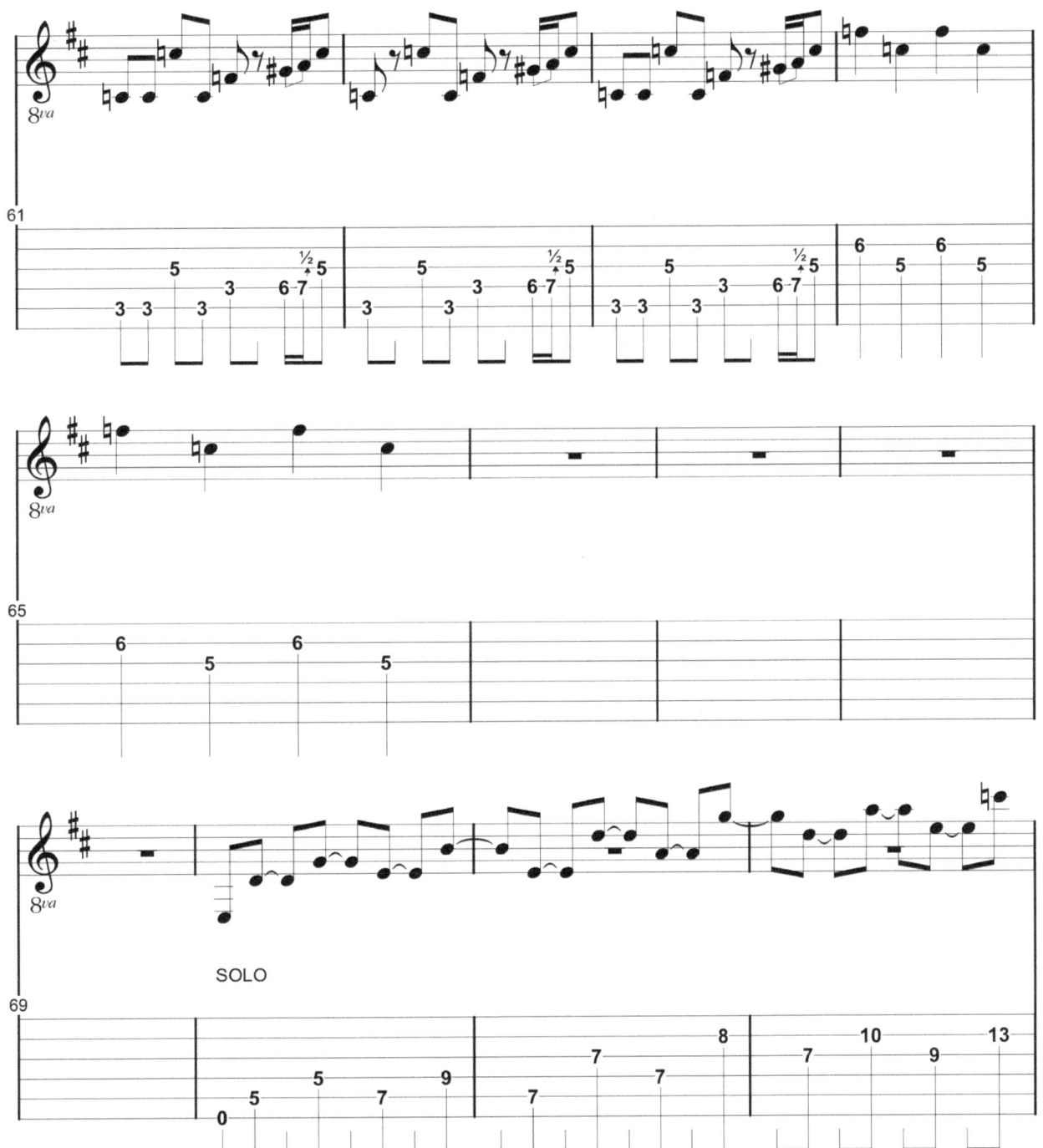

SATURDAY NITE IS DEAD
LEAD GUITAR -

SATURDAY NITE IS DEAD
LEAD GUITAR -

SATURDAY NITE IS DEAD
LEAD GUITAR -

SATURDAY NITE IS DEAD
LEAD GUITAR -

OUTRO

SATURDAY NITE IS DEAD
LEAD GUITAR -

SATURDAY NITE IS DEAD
LEAD GUITAR -

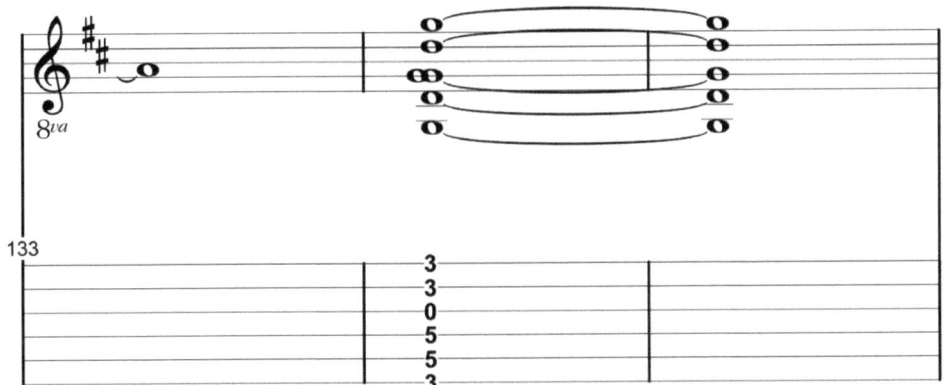

LOVE GETS YOU TWISTED

4/4

VERSE 1

E	B	/E	A	/C#m	/A	E	/

Love gets you twisted,   love gets you twisted   all the way   The

E	B	/E	A	/C#m	/A	E	/

hearts   are   enlisted,   the hearts are enlisted to break each day   I

BRIDGE 1

Pause…………..   Pause…………   Pause   Pause   Pause……………

G#m	F#m	/E	B	/C#m	A	/B	/

try to straighten out but I'm   too wrapped up to see   I don't know   how it's supposed to be

VERSE 2

E	B	/E	A	/C#m	/A	E	/

Love gets you twisted   love gets you twisted   inside out   I

E	B	/E	A	/C#m	/A	E	/

knew that it existed   I knew that it existed I had no doubt   When

BRIDGE 2

Pause…………   Pause…………   Pause   Pause   Pause……………

G#m	F#m	/E	B	/C#m	A	/ B	/

she's in my arms I get   tangled up it's true   I can't see   the other point of view

CHORUS

A	E	/C#m	F#	/

When love gets you twisted   love gets you twisted

2/4   4/4Pause…………..

E	/A	/B	A	/B	A	/

Love gets you twisted   Screw yourself up   screw yourself up

                              SOLO……………………………………………………

B	A	/C#m	/	/B	E	/

Screw yourself screw yourself up

………………………………………………………………………………………………

A	B	/C#m	/	/B	E	/

………………………………………

A	B	/

BRIDGE 3

Pause…………….	Pause………..	Pause	Pause	Pause…………..	
G#m	F#m /E	B /C#m	A	/B	/
try to straighten out but I'm	tangled up it's true	I can't see		the other point of view when	

CHORUS

				2/4	4/4 Pause……..	
A	E	/C#m	F#	/E	/A	/
Love gets you twisted		love gets you twisted		love gets you twisted		

B	A	/B	A	/B	A	/
Screw yourself up		screw yourself up		screw yourself, screw yourself		

OUTRO

FADE OUT

E	B	/C#m	B	/E	B	/C#m	B	/
		When love gets you twisted				When love gets you		

E	B	/C#m	B	/E	B	/C#m	B	/
Twisted		When love gets you twisted				When love gets you ….		

LOVE GETS YOU TWISTED
LEAD GUITAR

LOVE GETS YOU TWISTED
LEAD GUITAR -

81

LOVE GETS YOU TWISTED
LEAD GUITAR -

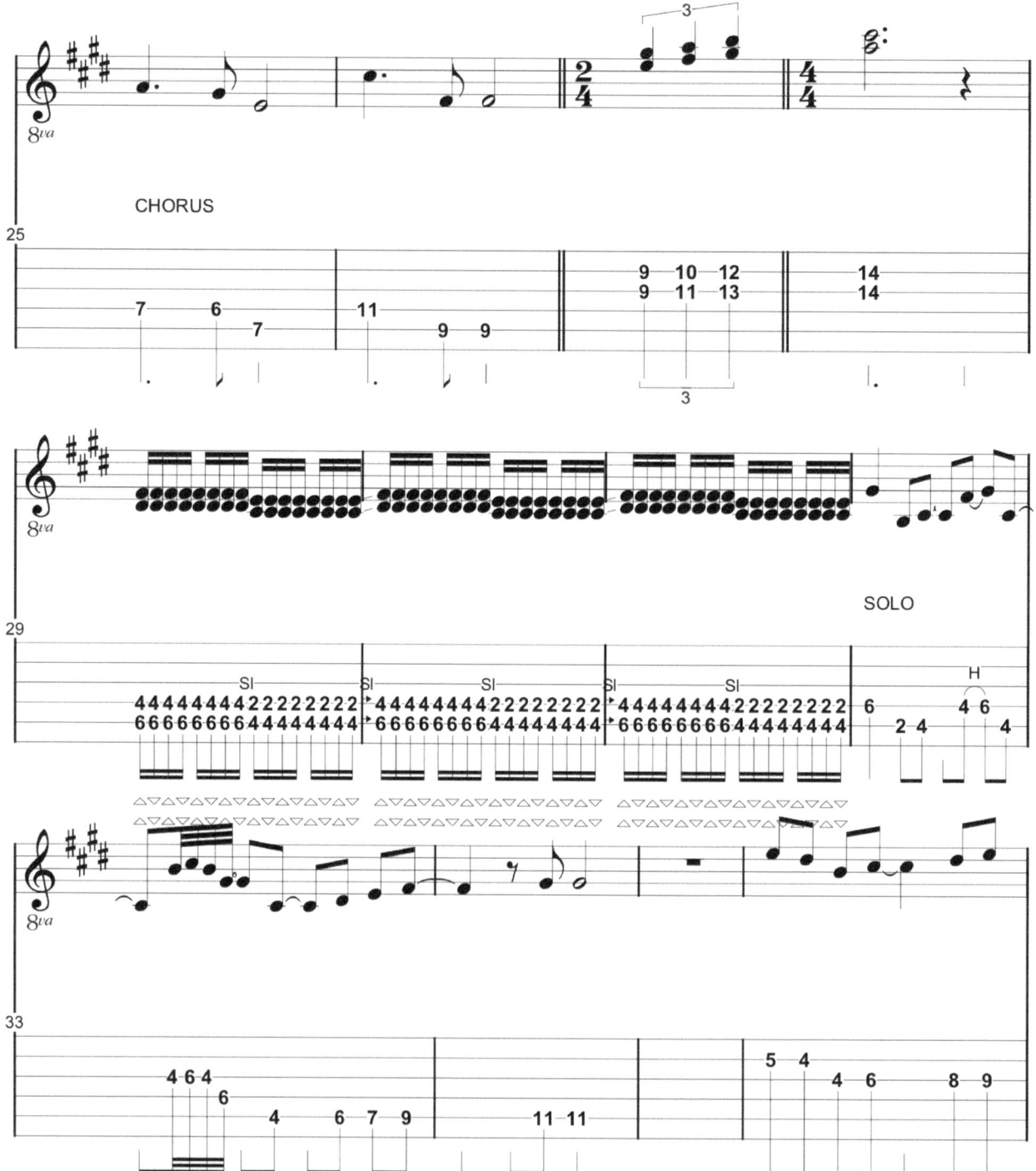

LOVE GETS YOU TWISTED
LEAD GUITAR -

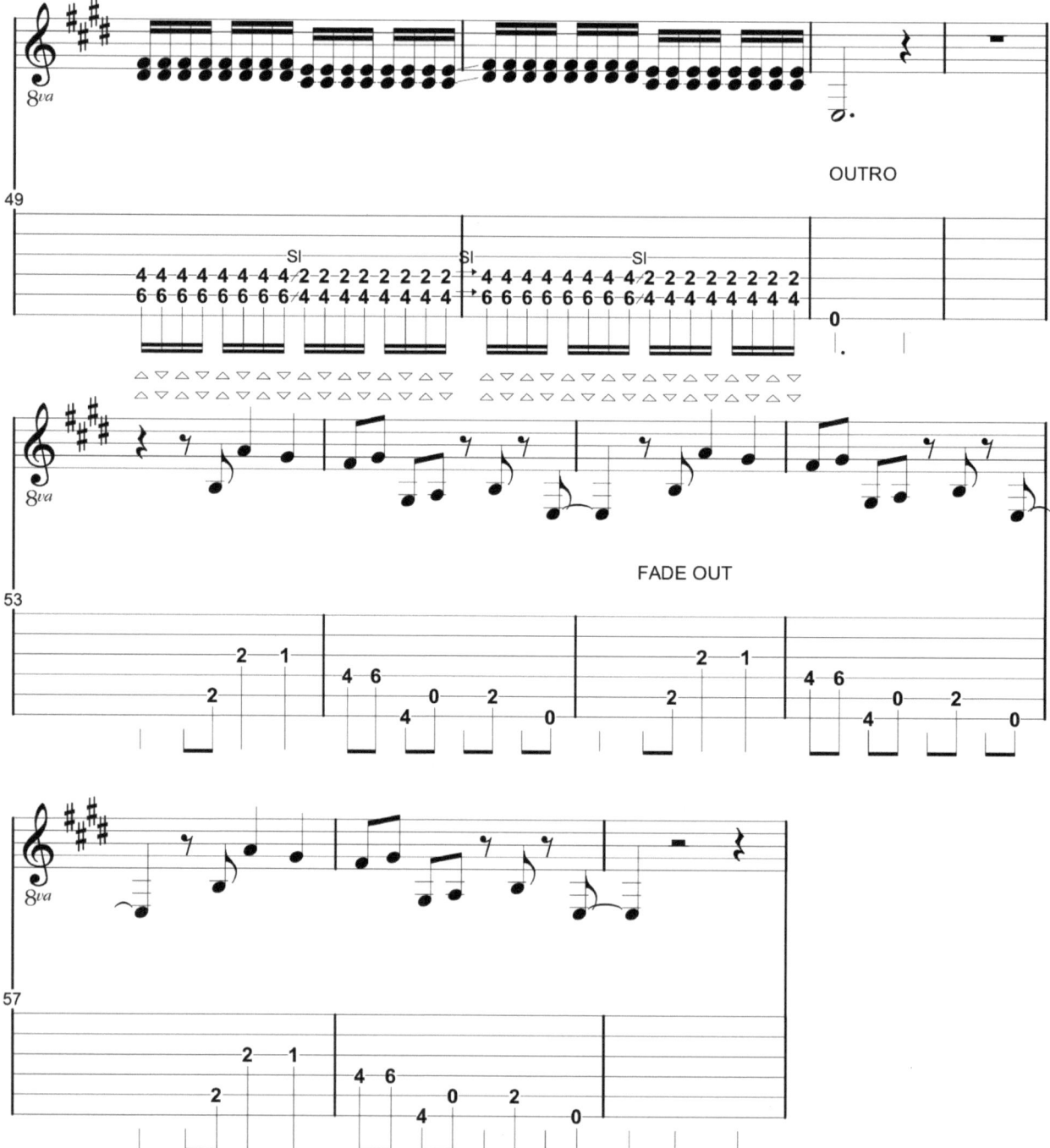

LOVE GETS YOU TWISTED
LEAD GUITAR -

PROTECTION

4/4

INTRO

/   E   Esus E /

F#m   /   E   Esus E /

F#m   /   E   Esus E /

VERSES 1 & 2

//:F#m   E   /A   D   /
     "So all of you be damned   we can't have heaven crammed"
     Every bomb is detonated   every switch is thrown and every

Bm   /   E   /
    Sir Winston Churchill said   I could have smacked his head
body tells me don't be scared   act as if you never cared

F#m   E   /A   D   /
    And all of those infected   waited to be collected I
    So I wear a blank expression to conceal my real impression

Bm   /   E   Esus E /
must get out at any price before the feeling gets too nice
Turn off all the information radios just pick up bad stations

CHORUS 1st time only

F#m   D   /A   E   Esus E /
  Just can't get, just can't get no   protection

F#m   D   /A   E   Esus E/
  Just can't get, just can't get no   protection

F#m   D   /A   E   /
  Just can't get, just can't get no   can't get no pro-

A   D   /A   D   /
tection,   Protection,   pro-
                        STOP

A   D   /F#m E   AA   ://
tection

CHORUS 2nd time

```
 F#m          D           /A        E    Esus E /
  Just can't get, just can't get no    protection

 F#m          D           /A        E    Esus E/
  Just can't get, just can't get no    protection

 F#m          D           /A        E               /
  Just can't get, just can't get no      can't get no pro-

 A           D           /A        D           /
 tection,               Protection,           pro-
                         2/4
 A           D           /F#m   E   /
 tection
```

BRIDGE 1

```
4/4
A5   C5   Dsus     /A5   C5   Dsus     /

A5   C5   Dsus     /A5   C5   Dsus     /
                                         So
A5   C5   Dsus     /A5   C5   Dsus     /
turn off the sound  I'm ready to go  down  I

A5   C5   Dsus     /A5   C5   Dsus     /
don't know myself,   I don't know you either  You're

A5   C5   Dsus     /A5   C5   Dsus     /
full of deceit       it's something I discovered  I

A5   C5   Dsus     /A5   C5   Dsus             /
know you've been mixing with big brother's brother   I say it ain't the

A5    C5    Dsus       /A5   C5   Dsus         /
knife thru the heart that tears you apart it's just the thought of someone    It's just the

A5   C5   Dsus     /A5   C5   Dsus     /
thought of someone    It's just the thought of someone    sticking it
```

F#m (alternating #5 and 5)............ /............................/
in,   sticking it in

VERSE 3 (as verses 1 & 2)

So if you think that's funny I'm not really laughing honey
Your love letters are confetti I ripped them up my hands were sweaty
And then those ghastly faces recur in nightmare places
Happy hour has come and gone much too short and much too long

CHORUS 3

```
F#m           D           /A        E   Esus E  /
  Just can't get, just can't get no    protection

F#m           D           /A        E   Esus E/
  Just can't get, just can't get no    protection

F#m           D           /A        E              /
  Just can't get, just can't get no     can't get no pro-

A             D           /A        D              /
 tection,                  Protection,             pro-

A             D           /E                       /
 tection,

F#m                       /G        A              /
```

BRIDGE 2 -OUTRO

```
B5   D5    E5       /B5    D5    E5         /

B5   D5    E5       /B5    D5    E5         /
Turn off all the  information radios  just pick up bad stations Pro-

B5   D5    E5       /B5    D5    E5         /
tection             Protection           It ain't the

B5   D5    E5            /B5    D5    E5    /
knife thru the heart that tears you apart  it's just the thought of someone sticking it in Pro-

B5   D5    E5            /B5   D5    E5     /
tection              Protection

B5   D5    E5       /B5    D5    E5         /
switch it off switch it off switch it off  switch  switch it off  switch it off   Pro-

B5   D5    E5       /B5    D5    E5         /
tection             Protection          you wanna

B5   D5    E5       /B5    D5    E5         /
hide? you want to hide? You want to hide  hide  hide hide Pro-
```

FADE OUT

```
B5   D5    E5       /B5    D5    E5    /B5    D5    E5    /
tection    yeah     Protection         Protection    Can't get Pro-

B5   D5    E5       /etc
tection
```

PROTECTION
ELECTRIC GUITARS

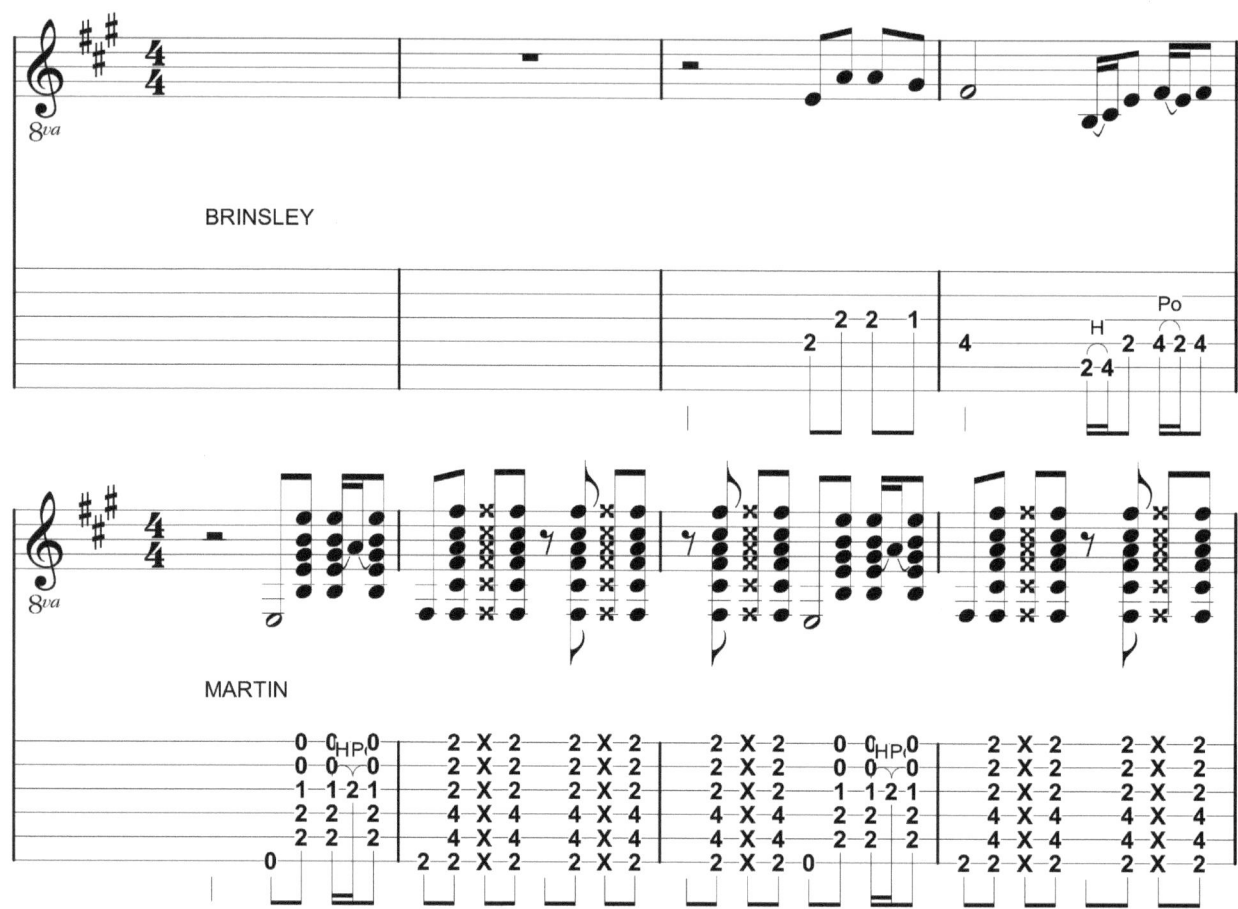

88

PROTECTION - ELECTRIC GUITARS

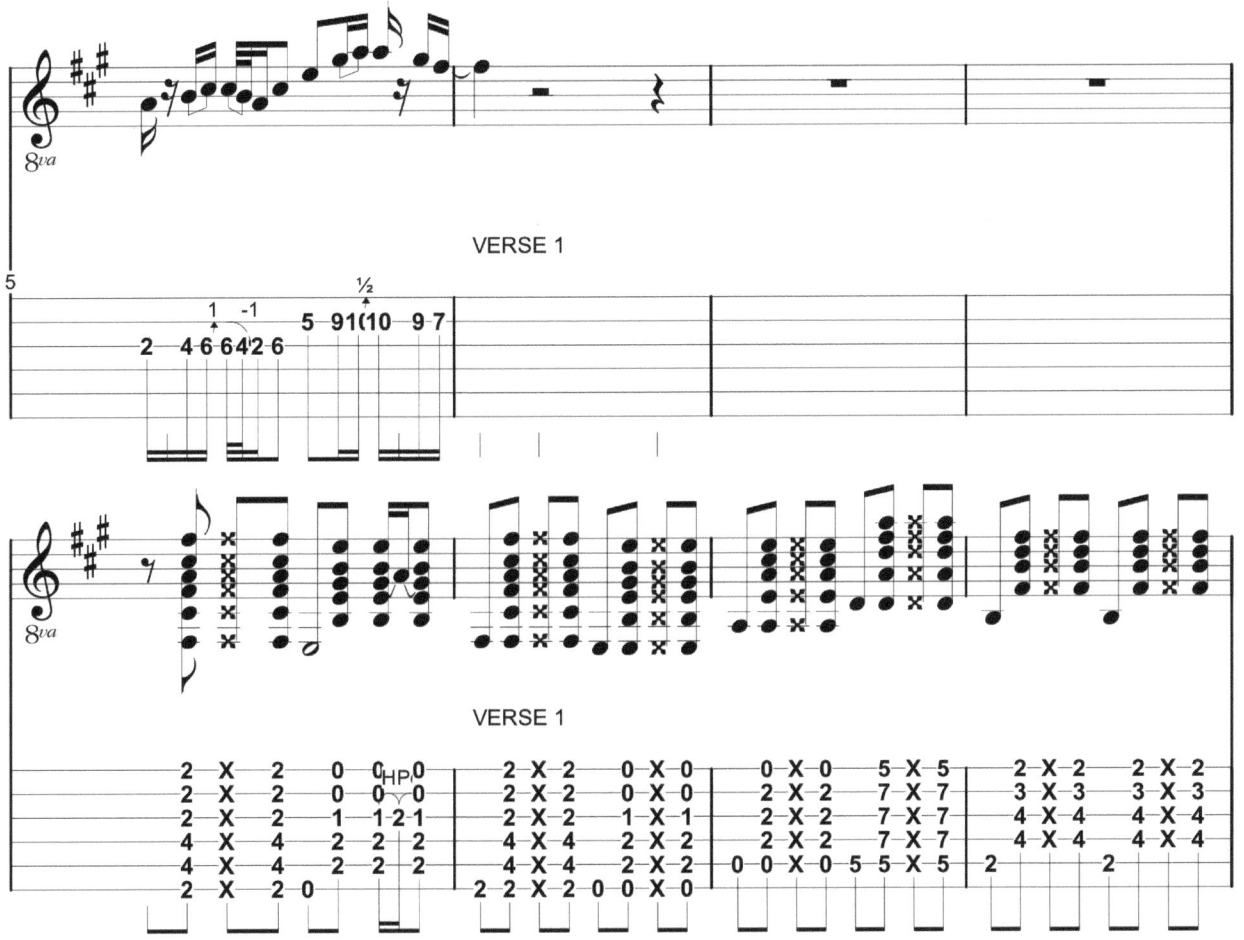

PROTECTION - ELECTRIC GUITARS

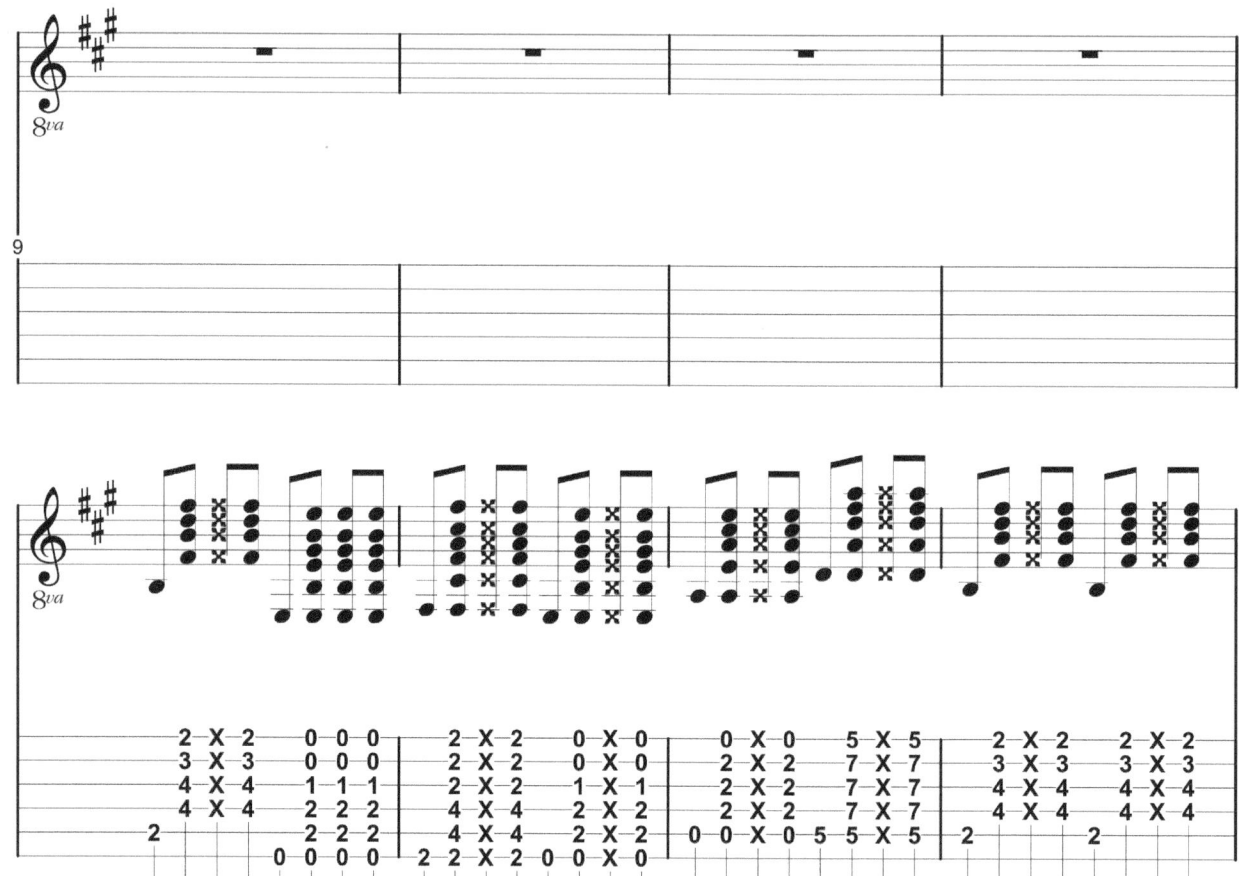

90

PROTECTION - ELECTRIC GUITARS

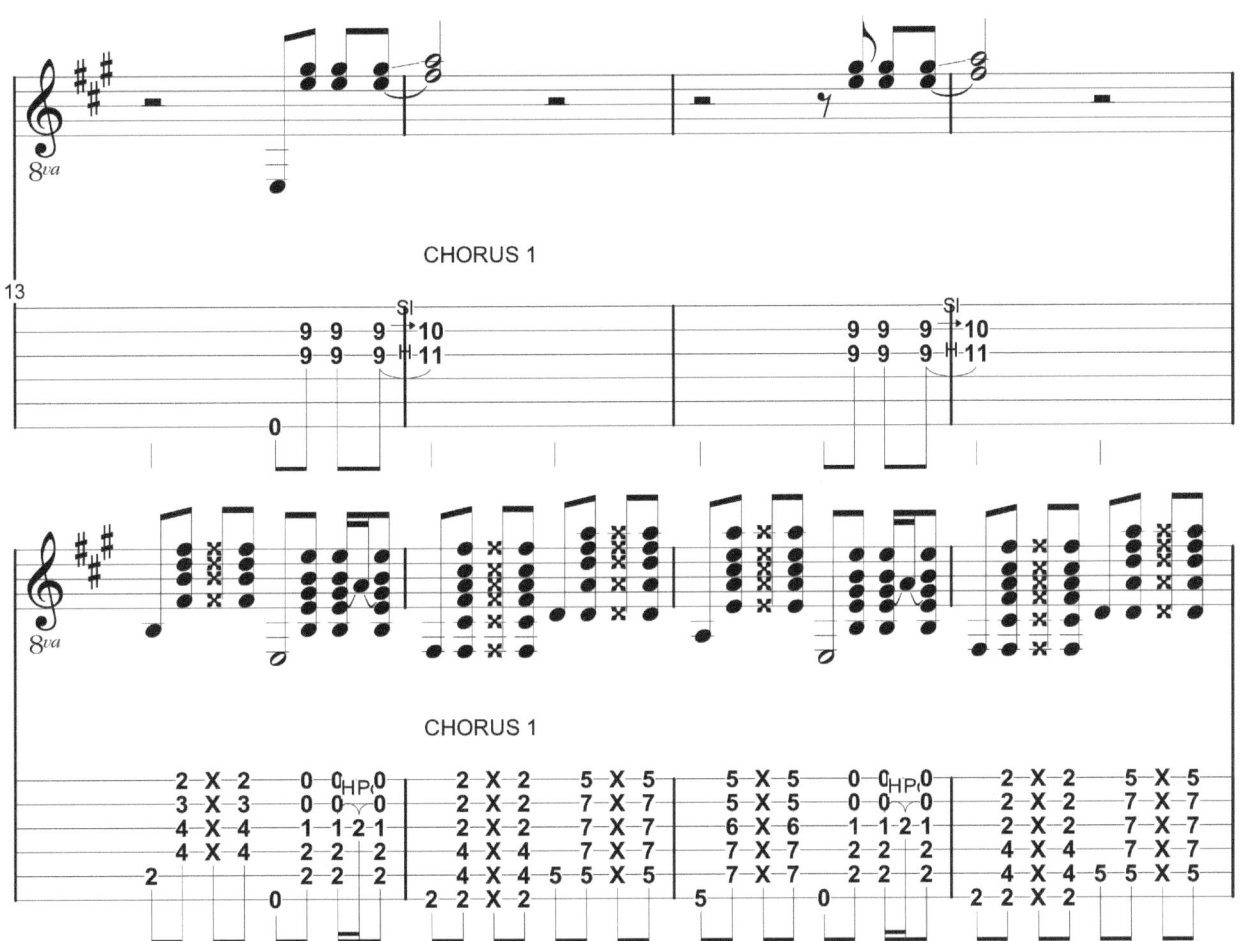

PROTECTION - ELECTRIC GUITARS

PROTECTION - ELECTRIC GUITARS

PROTECTION - ELECTRIC GUITARS

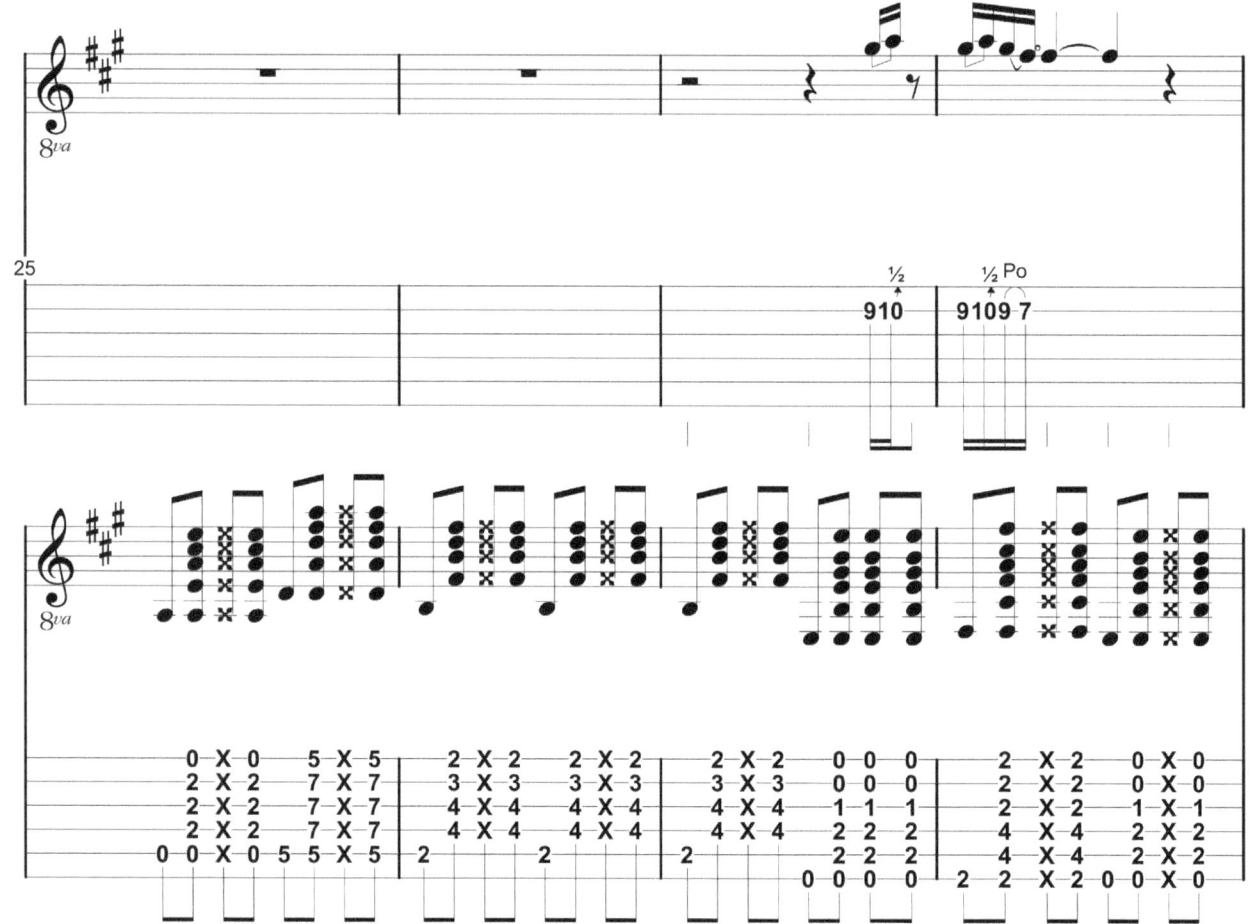

PROTECTION - ELECTRIC GUITARS

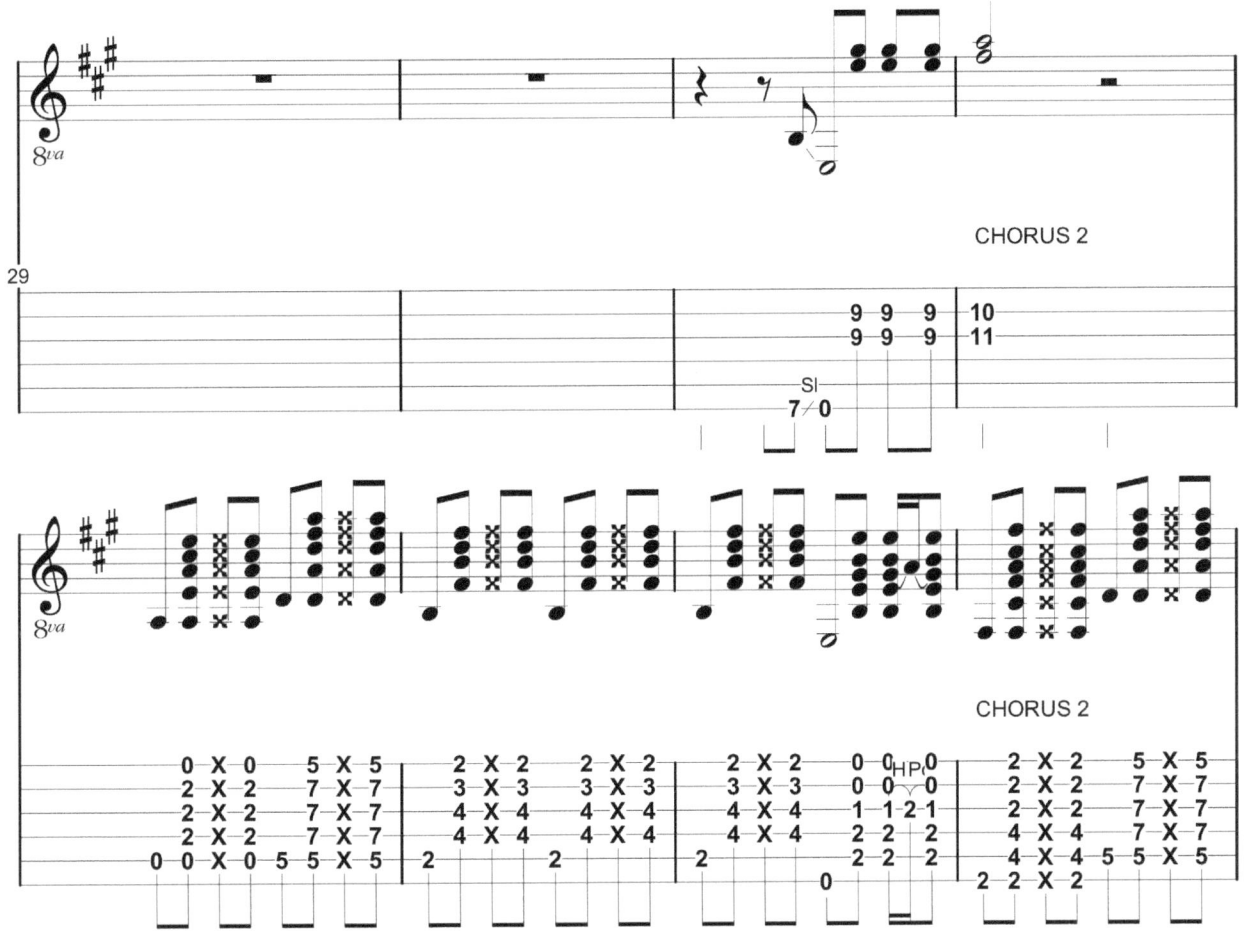

PROTECTION - ELECTRIC GUITARS

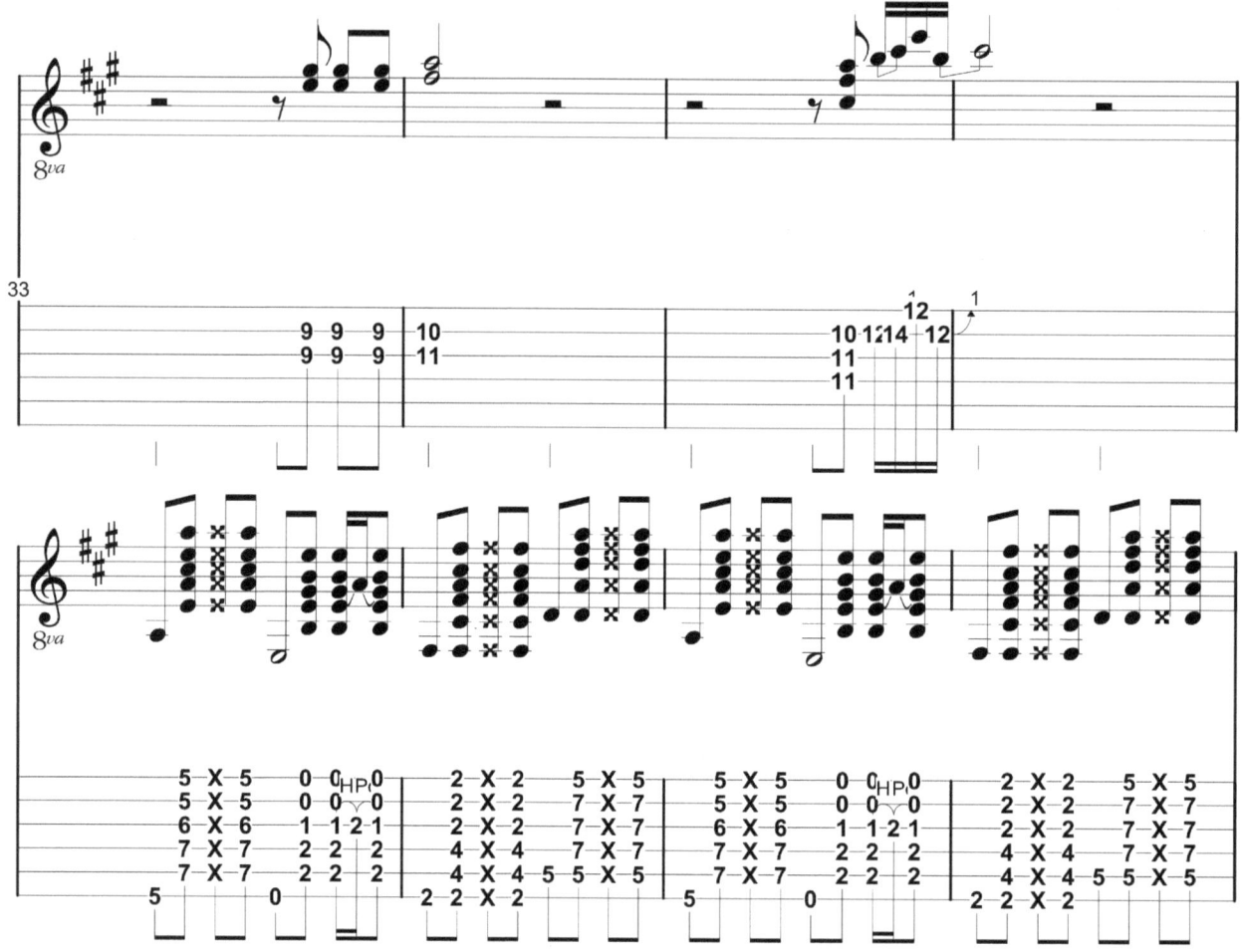

PROTECTION - ELECTRIC GUITARS

PROTECTION - ELECTRIC GUITARS

PROTECTION - ELECTRIC GUITARS

PROTECTION - ELECTRIC GUITARS

PROTECTION - ELECTRIC GUITARS

PROTECTION - ELECTRIC GUITARS

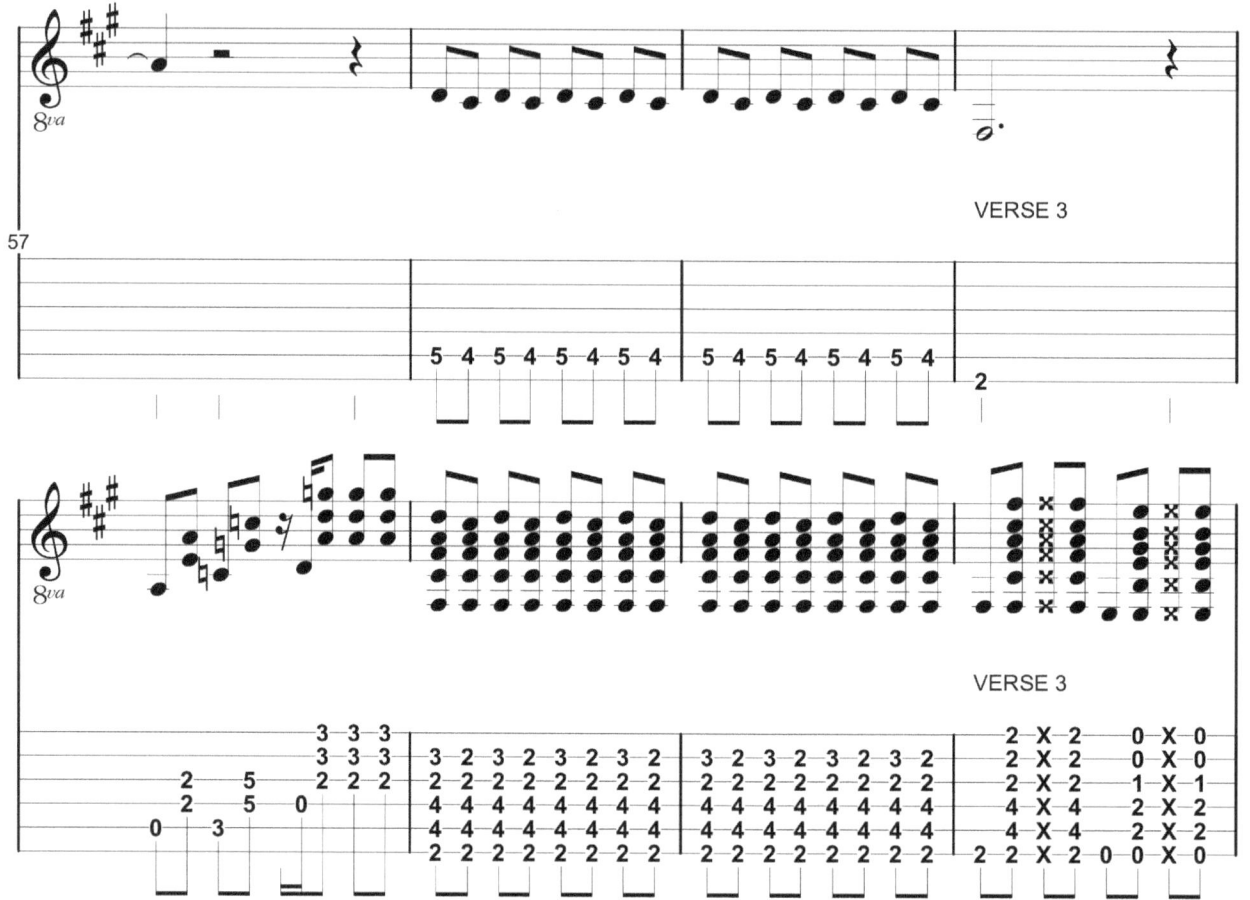

PROTECTION - ELECTRIC GUITARS

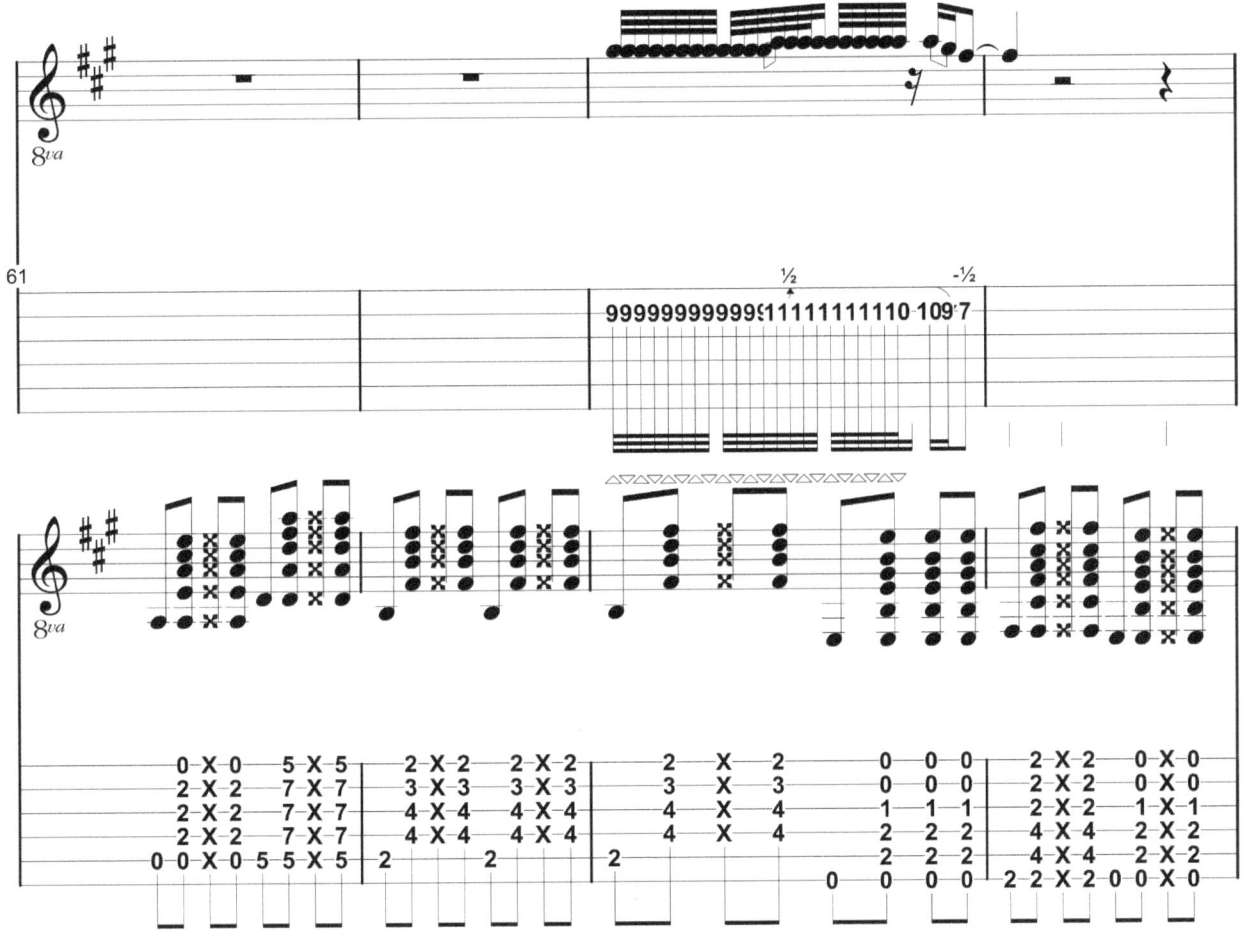

PROTECTION - ELECTRIC GUITARS

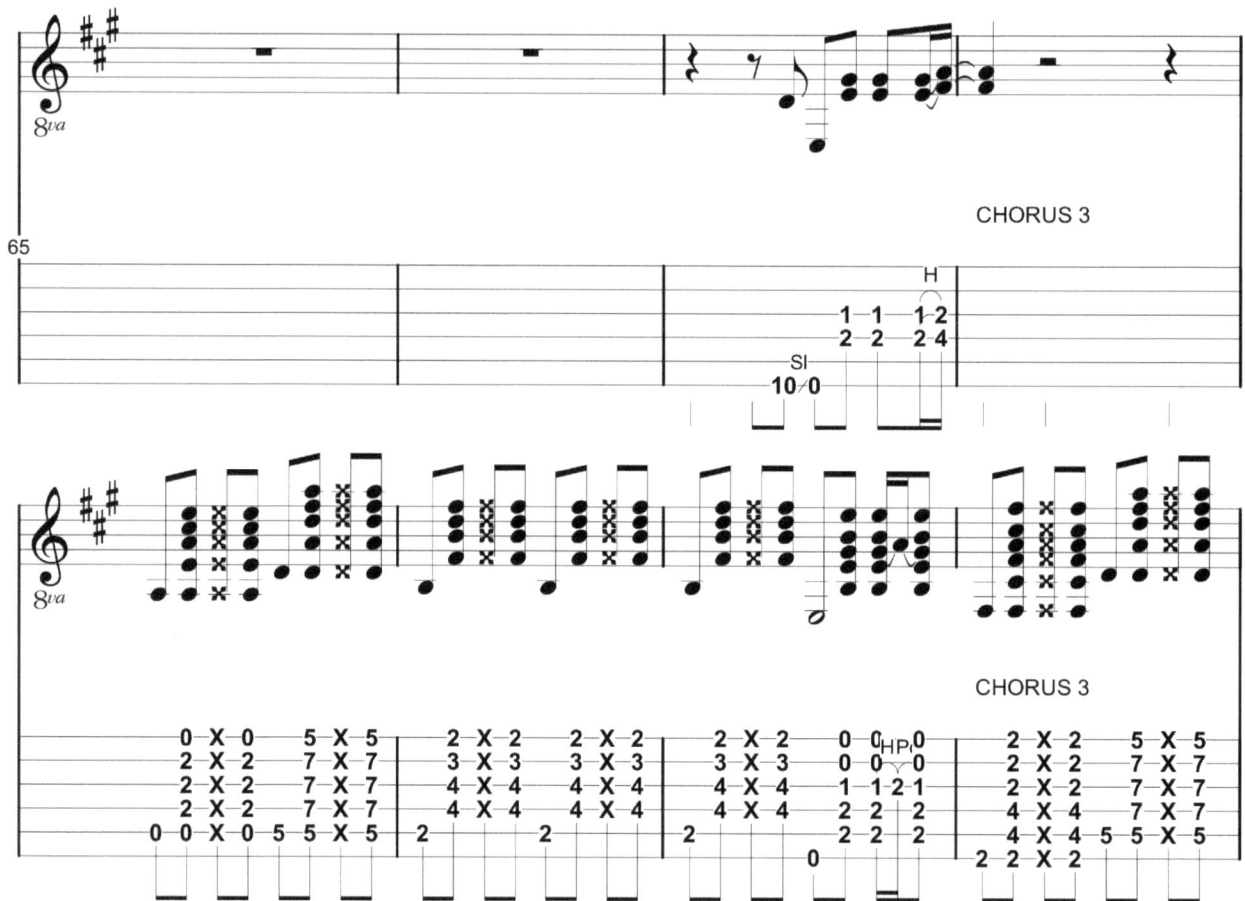

PROTECTION - ELECTRIC GUITARS

PROTECTION - ELECTRIC GUITARS

PROTECTION - ELECTRIC GUITARS

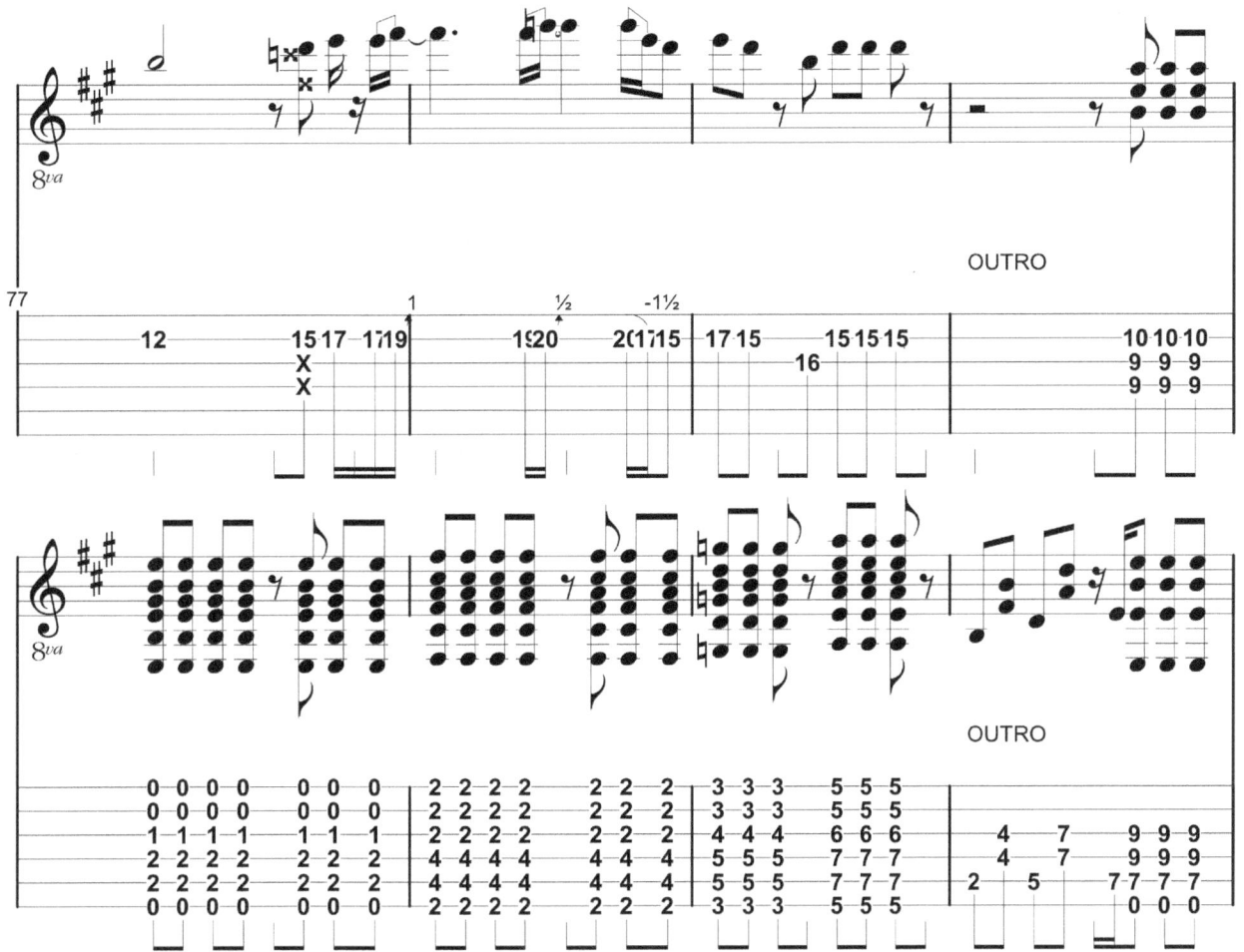

PROTECTION - ELECTRIC GUITARS

PROTECTION - ELECTRIC GUITARS

PROTECTION - ELECTRIC GUITARS

PROTECTION - ELECTRIC GUITARS

PROTECTION - ELECTRIC GUITARS

PROTECTION - ELECTRIC GUITARS

WAITING FOR THE UFO'S

4/4

INTRO

Pause	Pause	Pause	Pause	Pause	
D	/D	/Em	/G	A	/

Pause	Pause	Pause	Pause	Pause	
D	/D	/Em	/G	A	/

VERSES 1 & 2

```
//:D                    /          /Em              /G       A        /
    No-one can hide it      any... more       we know it's not imagining
    We're just a joke they sometimes  crack,   they'll get away with anything

D                       /          /Em              /G       A        /
    Even the skeptics  are un   sure        when they stop to think
    Earth government  is holding back,      they won't say a word
                                                        (and when do they ever)

G          /Bm                    /G              /Bm             /
    People are not worth a light now      they are obsolete
    Is that  a  light in the sky or     just a spark in my heart?

D          /A    Bm       /G            /A                    /
    We're dying to be  invaded and    put the blame on something concrete
    Can I accept this as evidence     or will that tear the whole act apart?
```

CHORUS 1 (1st time only)

```
G              /D              /Em              /D                /
Waiting for the ufos           waiting for the ufos       We are
                                                          2/4
A      G#      /G    F#m       /Em              /STOP           ://
waiting for the ufos    we know that they're  there
```

CHORUS 2 (2nd time)

```
G              /D              /Em              /D                /
Waiting for the ufos           waiting for the ufos       We are

A      G#      /G    F#m       /Bm              /                 /
waiting for the ufos    we know that they're  there             They're

Em             /                /
there
```

BRIDGE

```
C            G      /C           G     /Dsus  D          /Dsus  D              /
This new obsession  is turning us alien  too
                                              Pause
C            G      /C           G     /A                /
Much more resounding  my heart just stopped pounding  for you
```

ACAPPELLA SECTION

```
N.C.........................................................................
/              /              /              /              /
Waiting for the ufos          waiting for the ufos

.......................................................
                                                >
/              /              /              /D    A     /
Waiting for the ufos          we are waiting for the ufos
```

OUTRO

```
G                  /D           /Em              /D              /
Waiting for the ufos            waiting for the ufos

G                  /D           /Em              /D              /
Waiting for the ufos            we are waiting for the ufos   We are

G                  /D           /Em              /D              /
Waiting...........  waiting...........  Waiting  waiting    Waiting  waiting

G                  /D           /Em              /D              /
Waiting...........  waiting...........  Waiting  waiting    Waiting

G                  /D           /Em              /D              /
Waiting for the ufos            we are waiting for the ufos   We are

A       G#         /G    F#m    /Em                      /
waiting for the ufos  we know that they're  there eh eh eh eh ehe...........
```

WAITING FOR THE UFO'S
LEAD GUITAR

116

WAITING FOR THE UFO'S - LEAD GUITAR

CHORUS

117

WAITING FOR THE UFO'S - LEAD GUITAR

WAITING FOR THE UFO'S - LEAD GUITAR

WAITING FOR THE UFO'S - LEAD GUITAR

DON'T GET EXCITED

4/4

```
| | | | | |
 D       A   /N.C       /
                          There is
```

```
//:D      A    /E     D   /D      A    /E     D         /
   always     some advantage  to be wielded  and brought to bear       It's a
   running  round in circles           jump jump jumping out of cars   They put

    D       A    /E     D   /E                /
   lonely      occupation   keeping others out your hair  Your fingers
   animals     in cages              specimens in jars    Somehow

    D       A    /E     D   /D      A    /E     D         /
   on      all the switches  you talk in whispers  you're talking soft   You know
   now     there's no temptation  baby nails  digging under skin         It don't

    D       A         /E    D   /E                /
   all      my favourite pitches   you know what gets me off   But
   give me  the right sensation    it's just another thing     You

    D              /E          /D                    /E   F#m    /
   try to reach a vital part of me   My interest level's dropping rapid - ly    It's
   try to reach a vital part of me   My attention span is dropping rapid-ly     It's
```

1st TIME ONLY
```
                         | | | | | |
 D         /E      /D           A      /N.C        ://
 all excuses baby  all a stall I just  don't  get  excited        I've been
```

2nd TIME
```
                         | | | | | |
 D         /E      /D           A     /E  F#m  D  A  /
 all excuses baby  all a stall we just don't get excited   Don't get excited no
```

```
| | | | | |    2/4         4/4
 D          A    /E  F#m  /Asus   Asus  /Asus   Asus   /
 Don't get excited   Don't get excited
```

122

```
G#m                    /E                 /
Talk about it talk about it all night long

G#m                    /E                         /
Think about it think about it nothing's wrong don't get ex-

G#m                /E              /G#m              /E              /
-cited                    Don't get excited                 Don't get ex-

G#m       (sus4)   /E              /G#m      (sus4)  /E              /
-cited                    Don't get excited                 Don't get ex-

G#m       (sus4)   /E              /G#m      (sus4)  /E              /
-cited                    Don't get excited                 Don't get ex-
```

INSTRUMENTAL

```
E                    /                   /
-cited

D              /E           /D            /E            /


                                    | | | | | |   | | | | | |
D              /E           /D       A  /D       A  /

| | | | | |
D       A     /
              Baby

D    A   /E       D    /D   A  /E       D         /
listen   without thinking.  You better obey   without demands   Now don't get

D    A   /E       D    /E                /
edgy    and don't start blinking and don't start making any plans   You

D          /E         /D          /E      F#m     /
try to reach a vital part of me.  My interest level's dropping rapid - ly   It's

                              | | | | | |
D          /E         /D      A  /E   F#m D  A  /
all excuses baby  all a stall we just don't get excited   Don't get excited no

| | | | | |                  | | | | | |    | | | | | |
D      A  /E  F#m D  A  /D         A  /D         A  /
Don't get excited   Don't get excited no  Don't get excited.  Don't get excited.

| | | | | |    | | | | | |
D      A  /D       A  //
Don't get excited.  Don't get excited!
```

DON'T GET EXCITED
ELECTRIC GUITARS

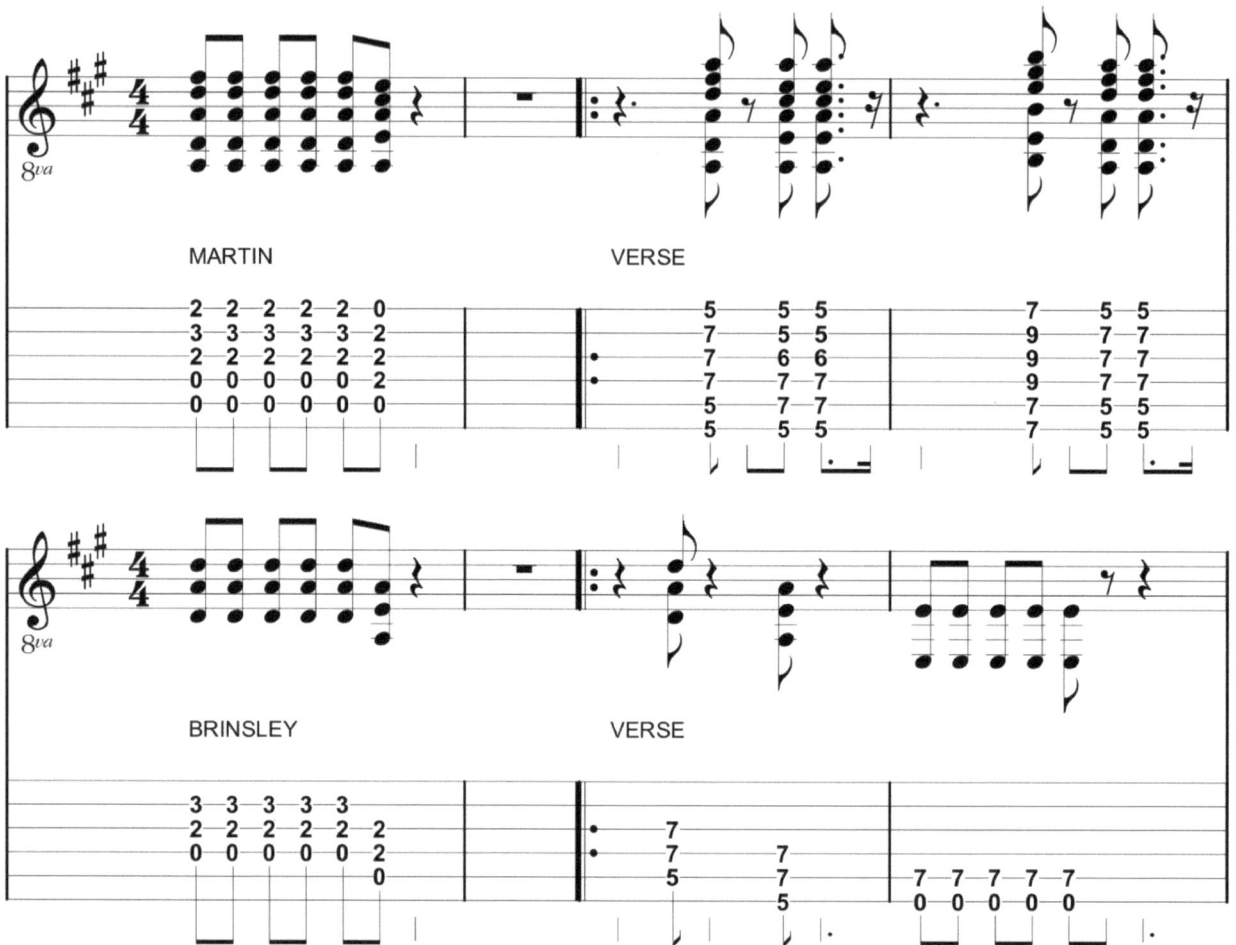

DON'T GET EXCITED - ELECTRIC GUITARS

DON'T GET EXCITED - ELECTRIC GUITARS

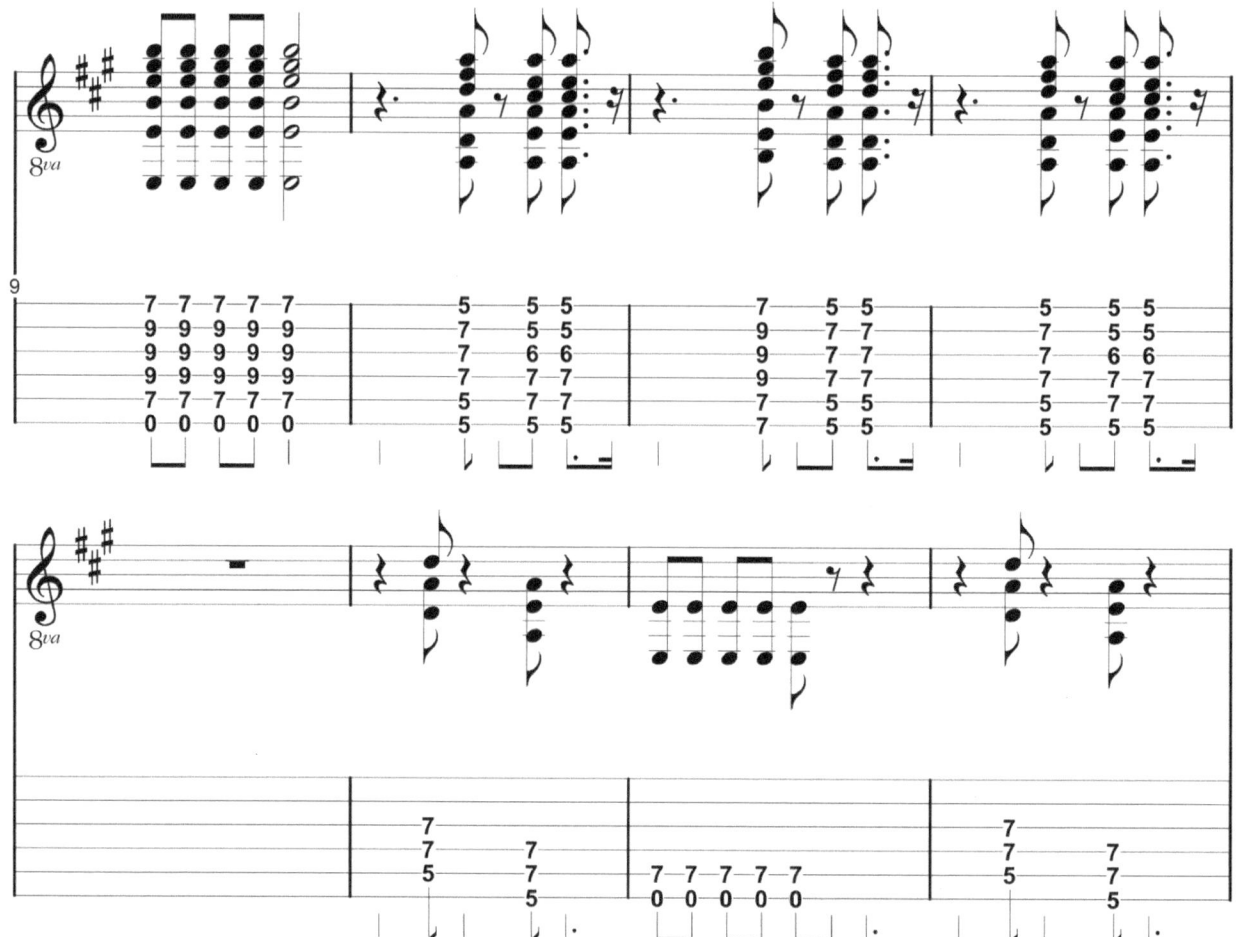

DON'T GET EXCITED - ELECTRIC GUITARS

DON'T GET EXCITED - ELECTRIC GUITARS

DON'T GET EXCITED - ELECTRIC GUITARS

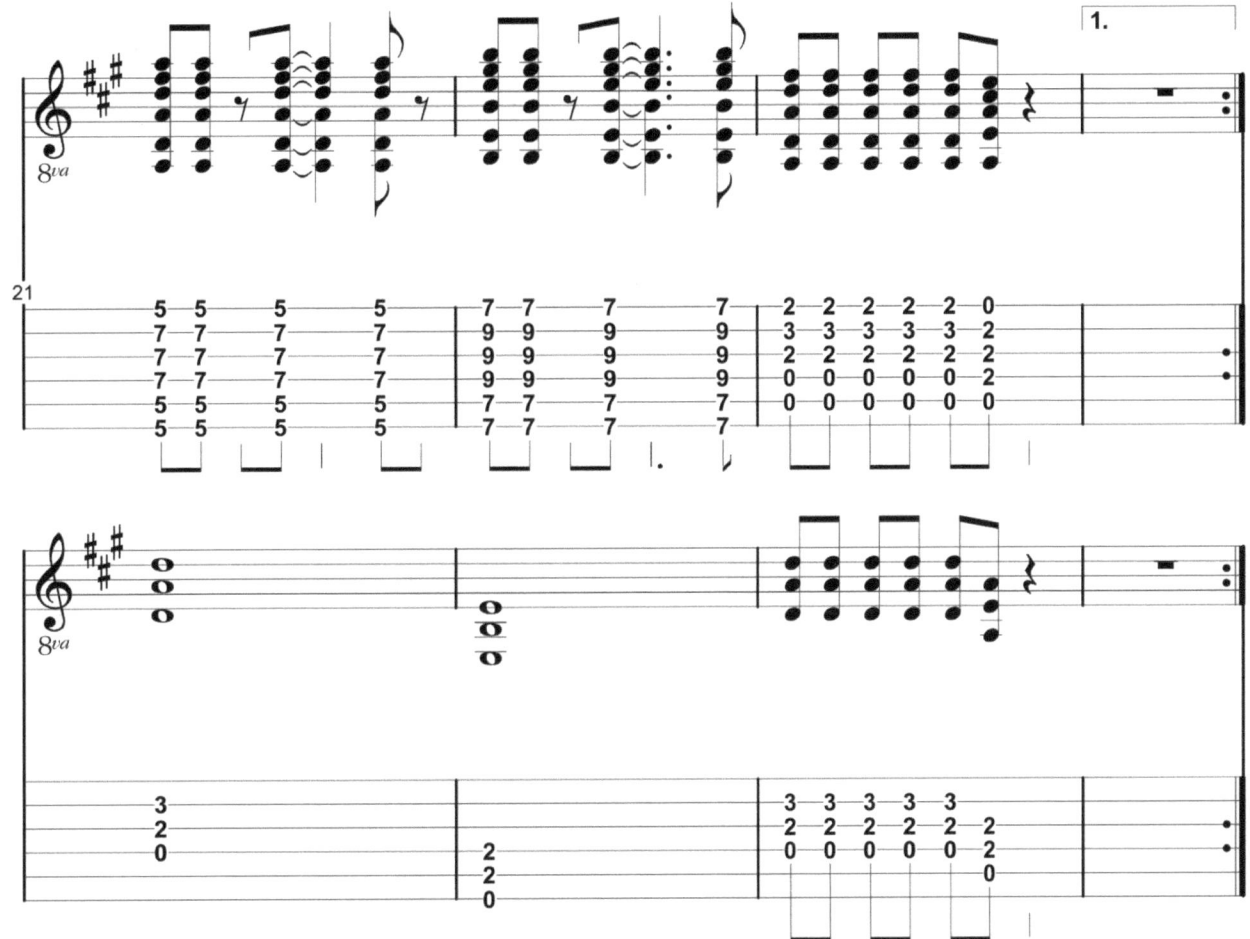

DON'T GET EXCITED - ELECTRIC GUITARS

DON'T GET EXCITED - ELECTRIC GUITARS

DON'T GET EXCITED - ELECTRIC GUITARS

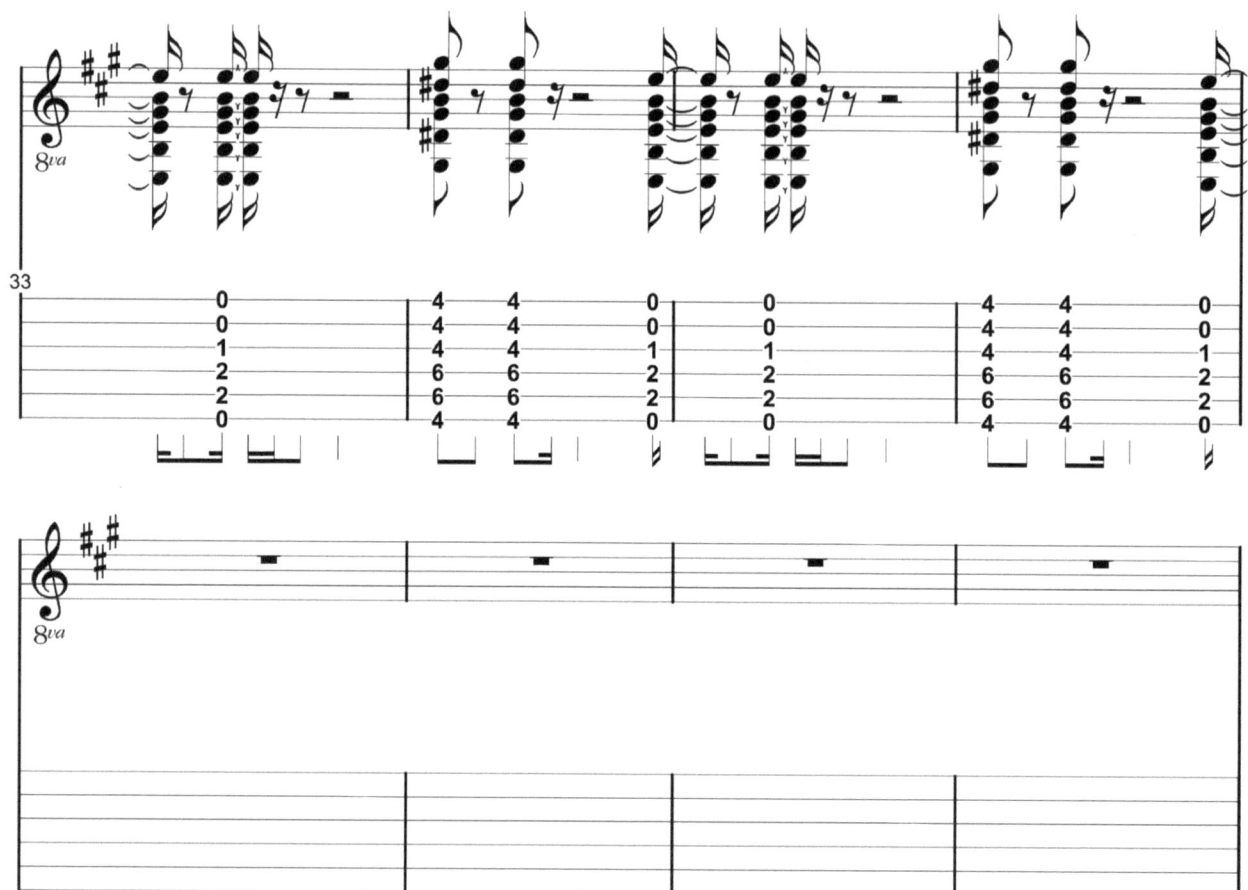

132

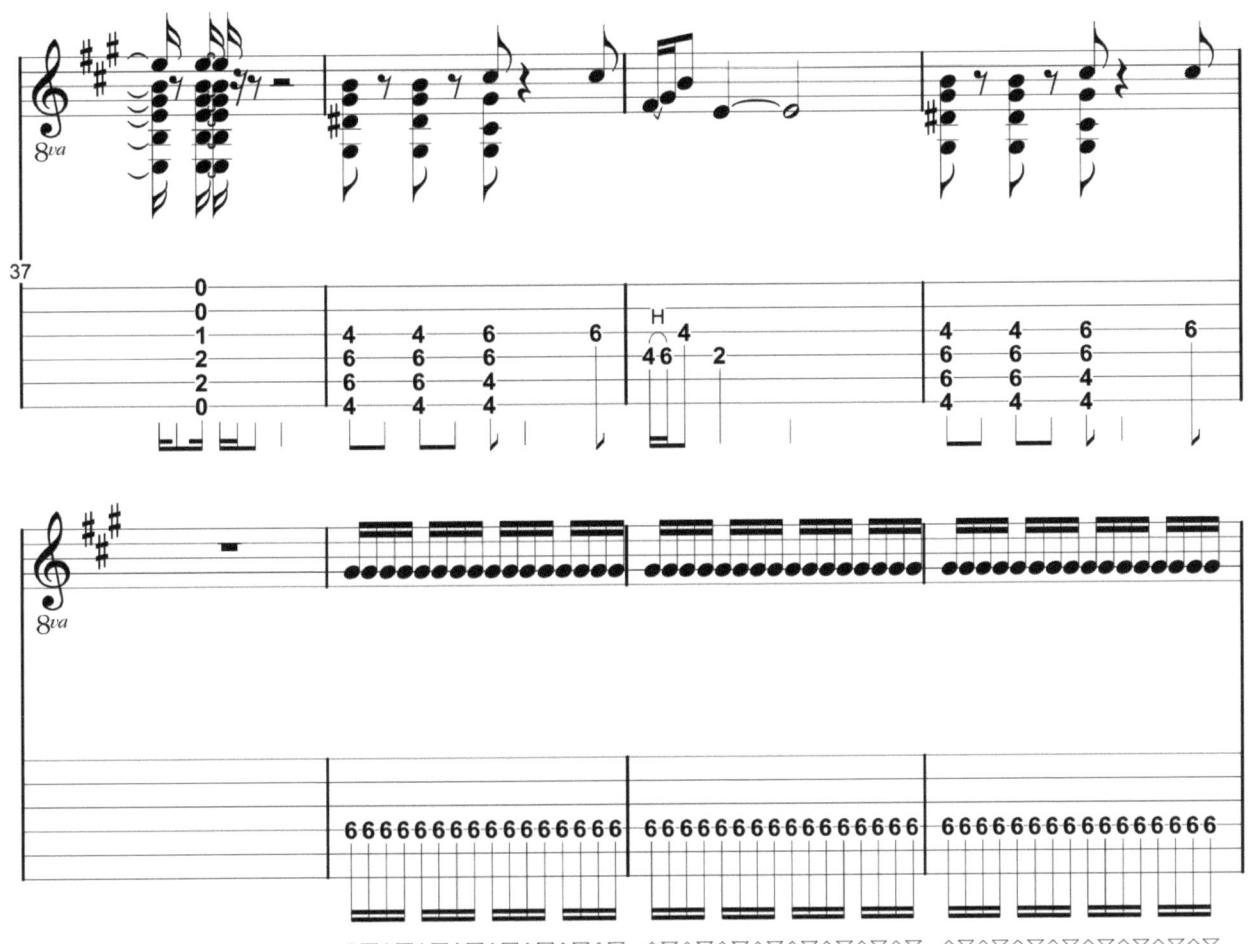

DON'T GET EXCITED - ELECTRIC GUITARS

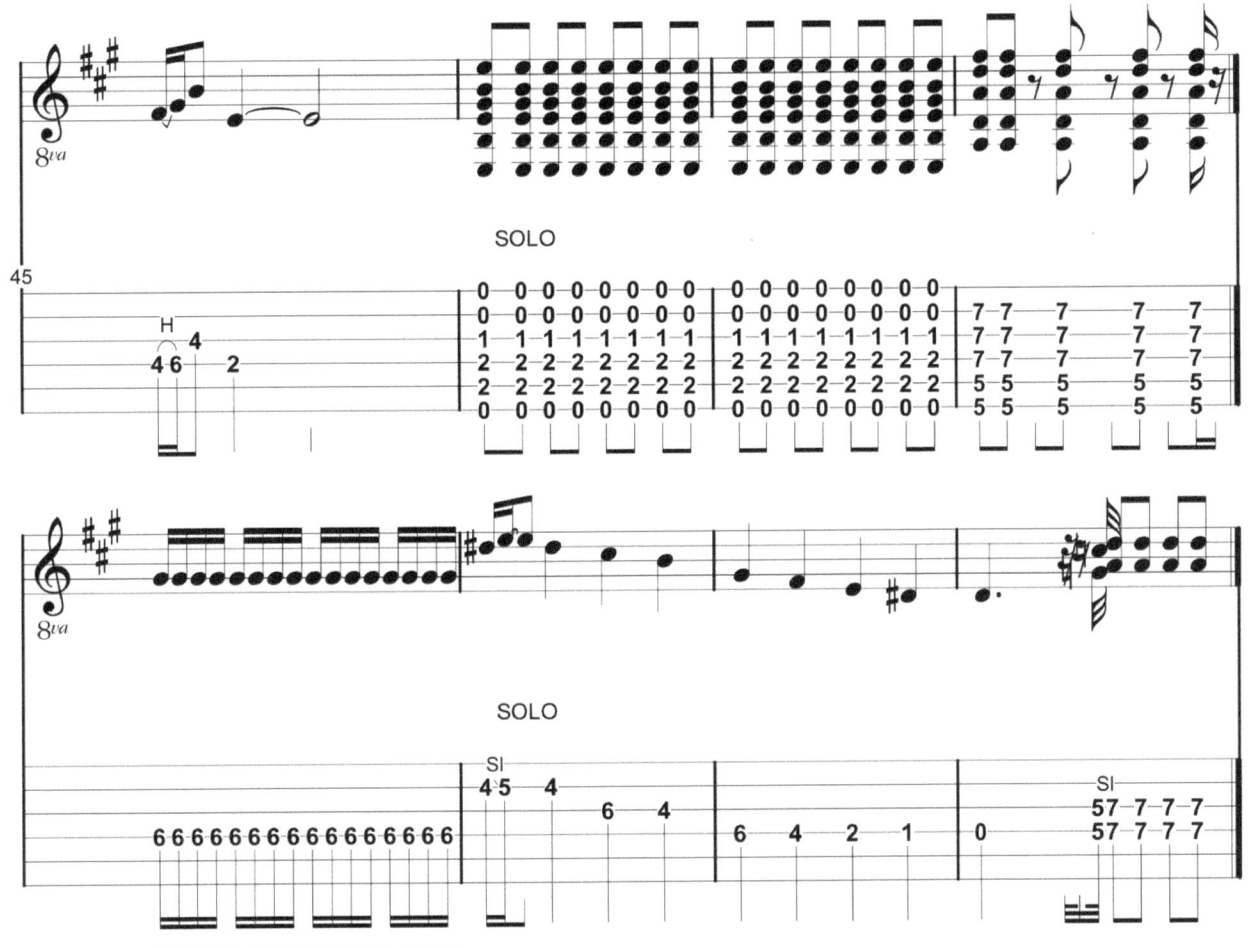

DON'T GET EXCITED - ELECTRIC GUITARS

DON'T GET EXCITED - ELECTRIC GUITARS

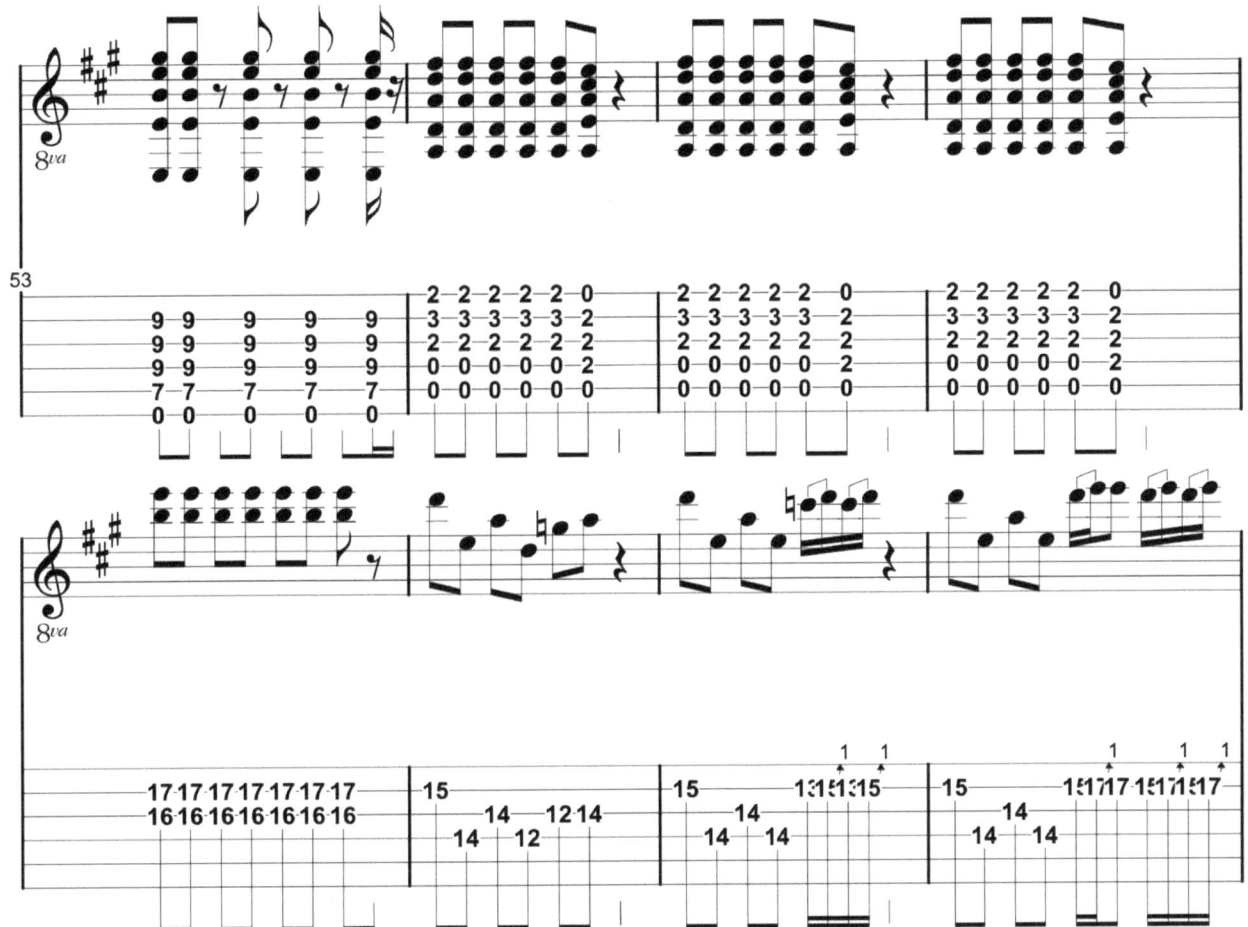

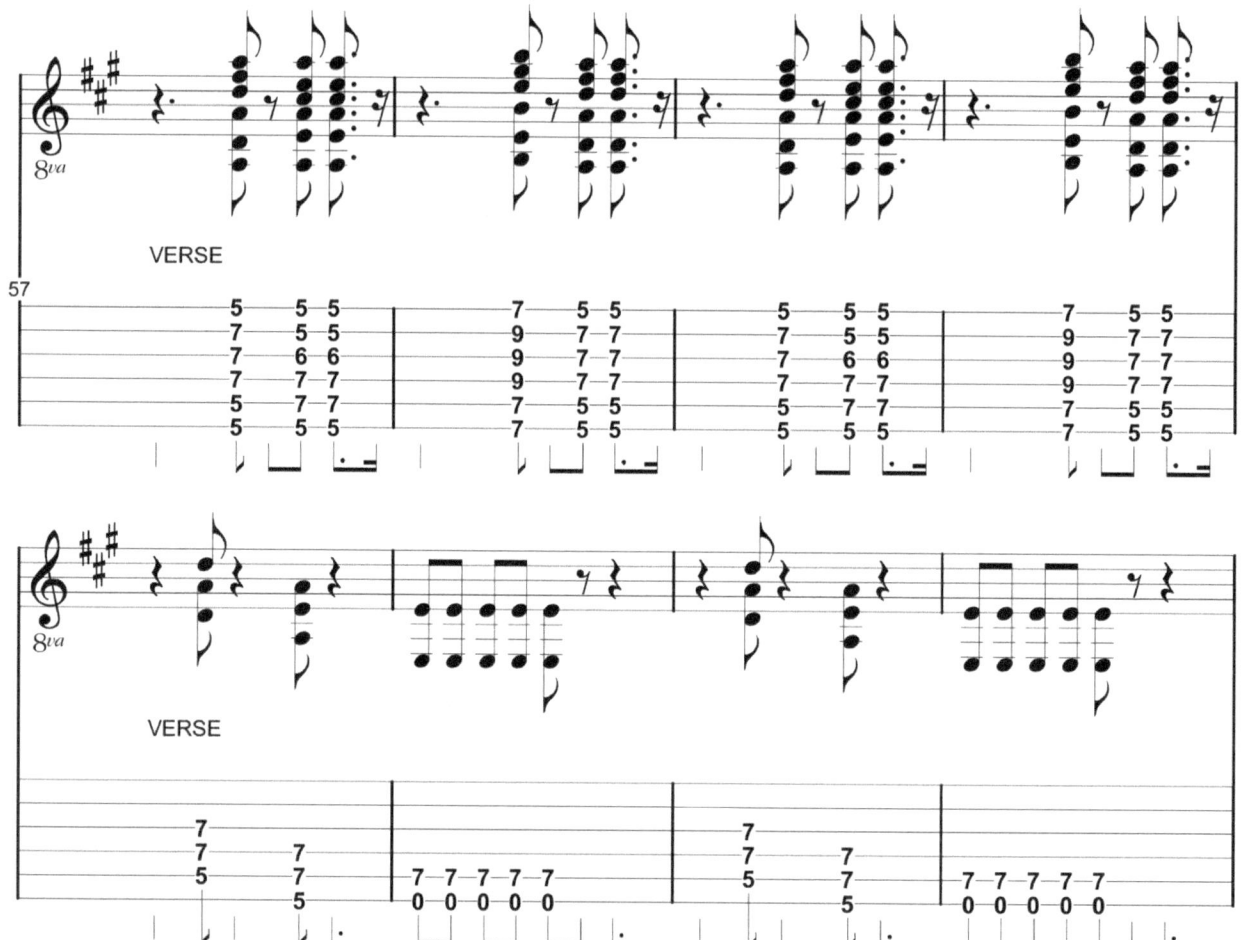

DON'T GET EXCITED - ELECTRIC GUITARS

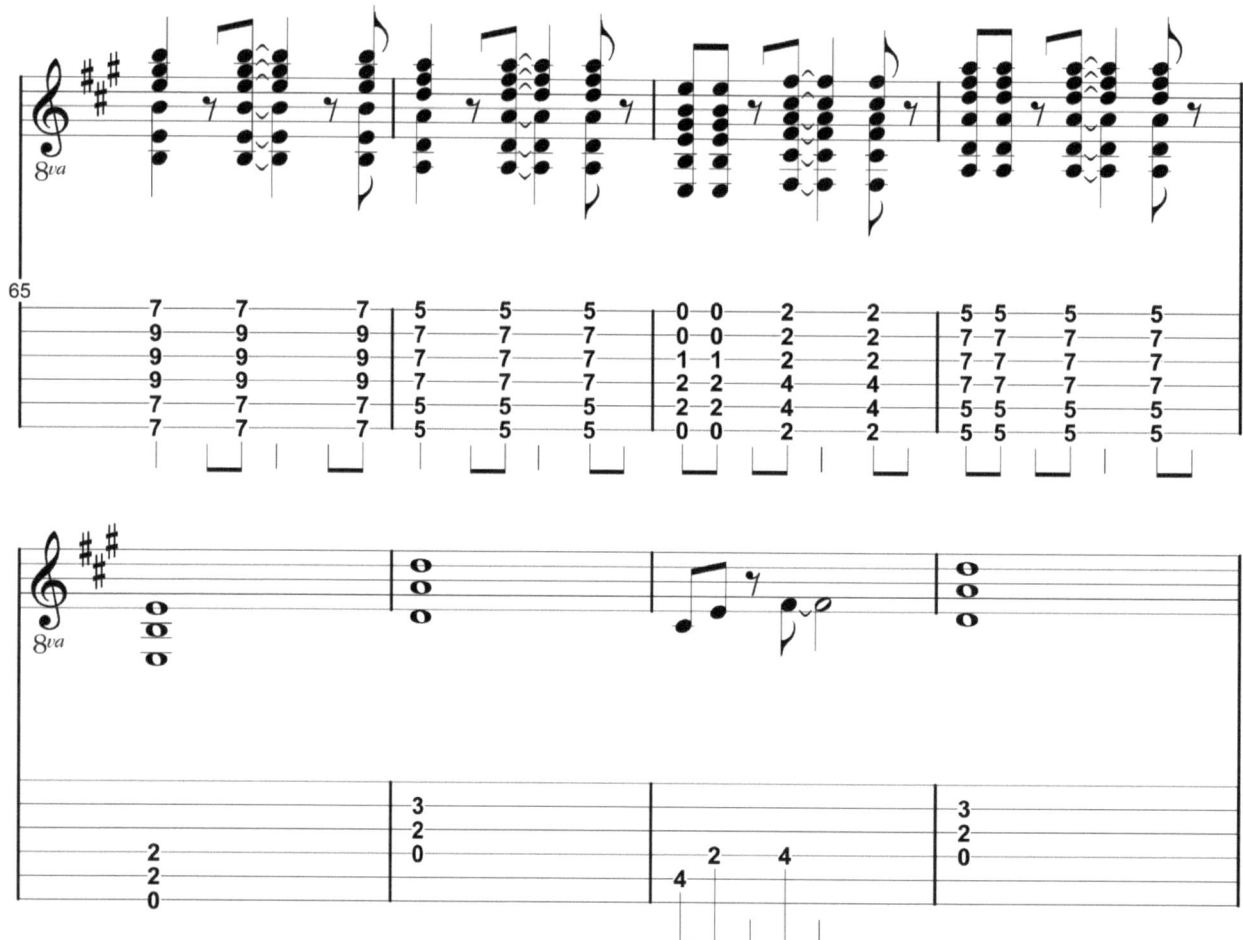

DON'T GET EXCITED - ELECTRIC GUITARS

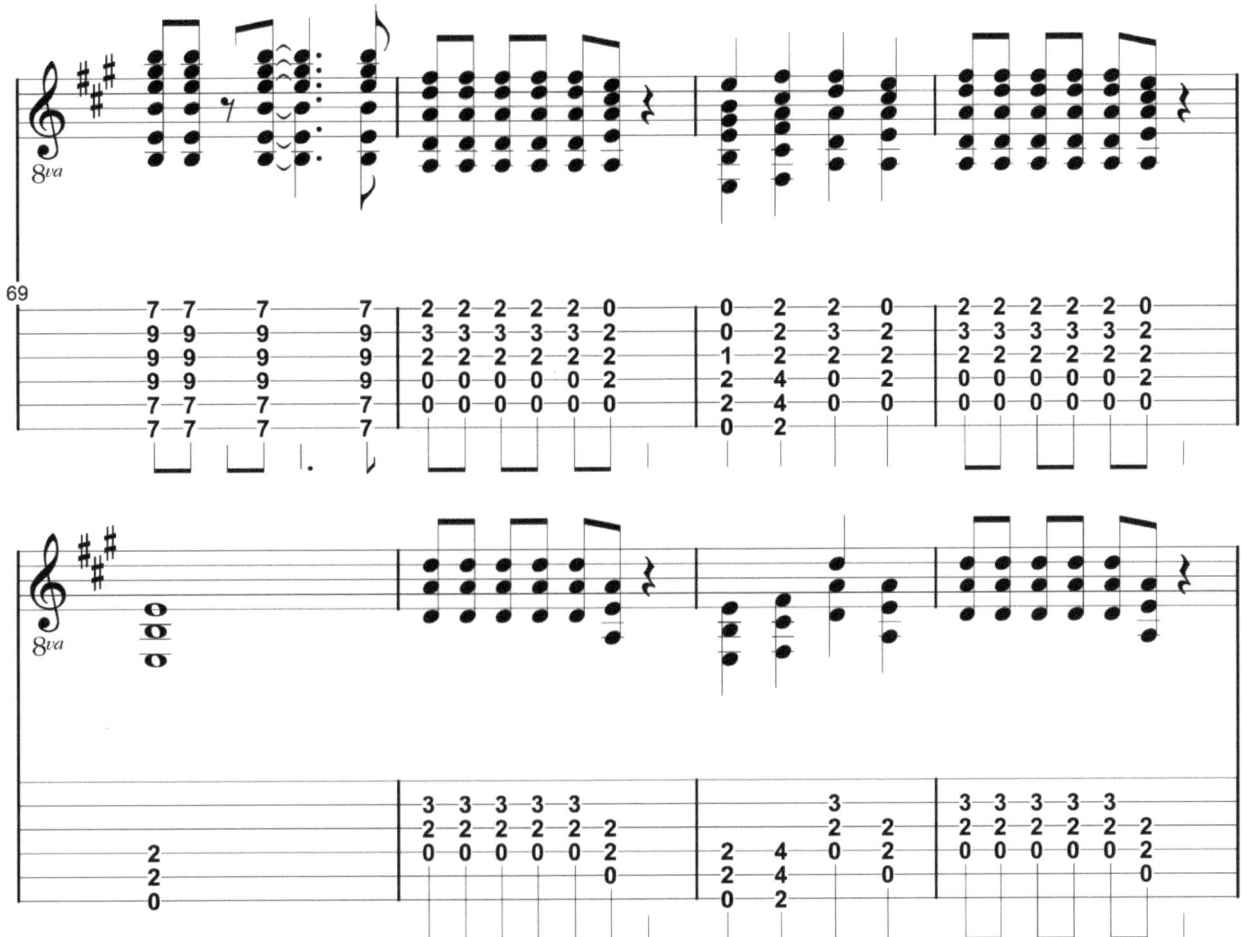

141

DON'T GET EXCITED - ELECTRIC GUITARS

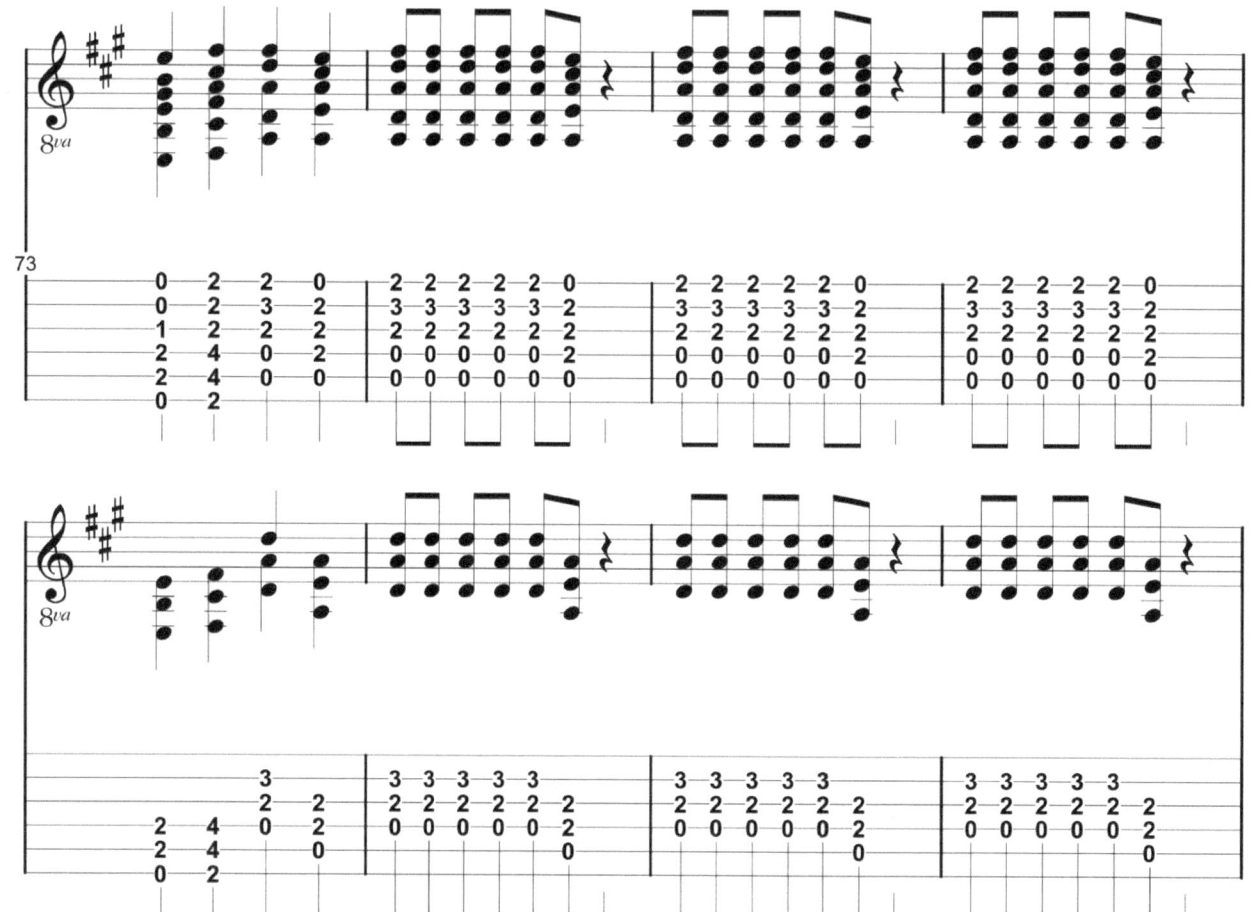

DON'T GET EXCITED - ELECTRIC GUITARS

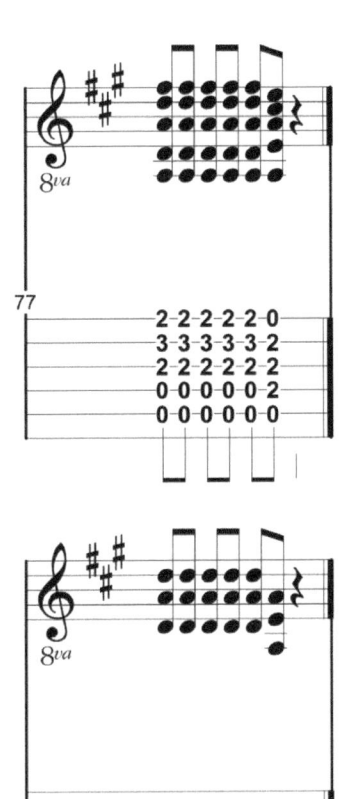

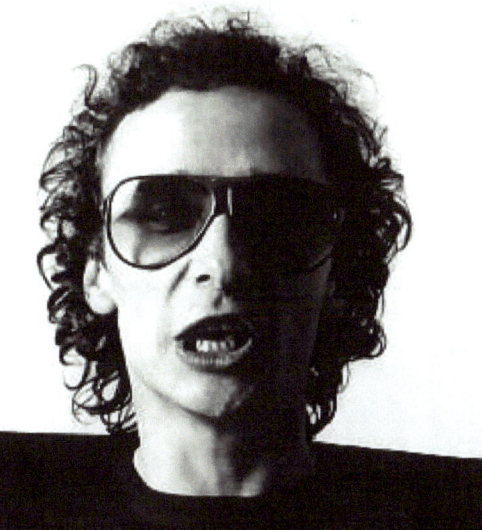

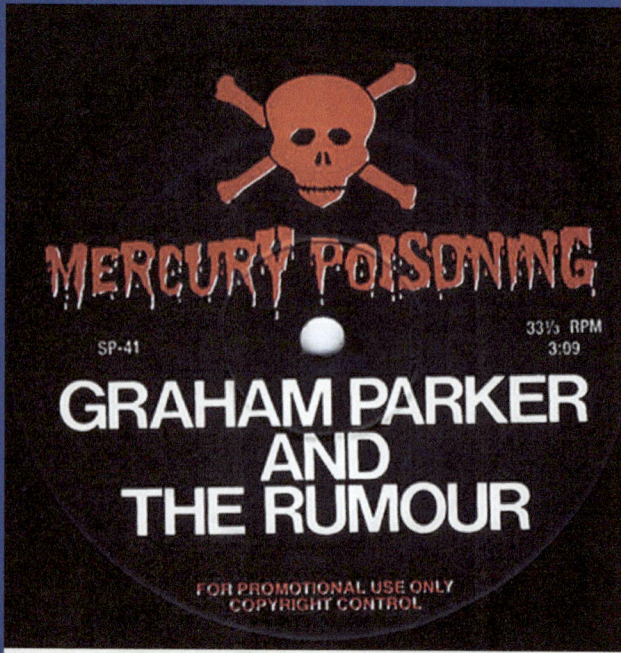
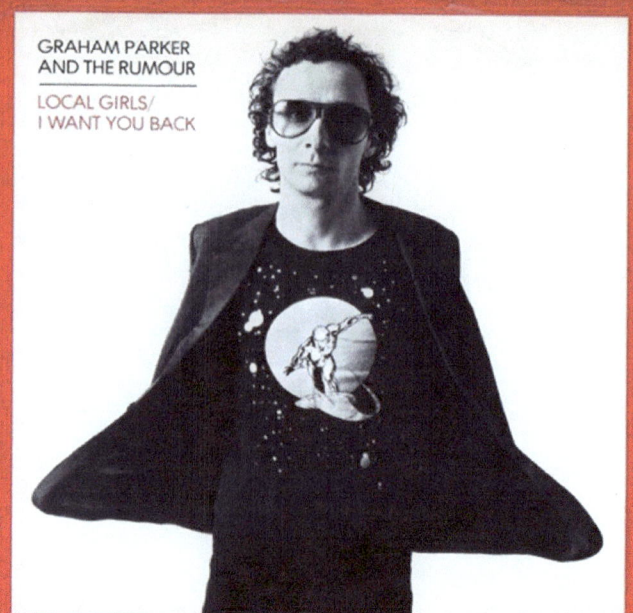

Left to right: Michael Jackson, Graham Parker, Lene Lovich

MERCURY POISONING

4/4

INTRO

C   G   /Bb   F   / X 5

VERSE 1 & 2

//:C   G   /Bb   F   /C   G   /Bb   F   /
   No more pretending now, the albatross is dying in its nest   The
   boys and me are getting   real well known around town   But

C   G   /Bb   F   /Am   /   /
company is crippling me, the worst trying to ruin   the best,   the best
every time we try to spread the action someone always brings it down, down

Bb   /C   /Bb   /C   /
   Their promotion's so lame.   They could never ever take it to the real ball game
   I ate the orange and I don't feel well   For them it's inconvenience for me it's hell   Their

                                              >
F   C   /G   /F   C   /G   /
   Maybe they think I'm a pet   Well I've got all the diseases I'm breaking out in sweat,
geriatric staff think we're freaks   They couldn't sell kebabs to the Greeks   the geeks

G   /
   you bet,   'cause
   Action speaks 'cause

CHORUS

C   G   /Bb   F   /C   G   /Bb   F   /
   I've got,   Mercury Poisoning   It's fatal and it don't get better

C   G   /Bb   F   /Bb   /
   I've got,   Mercury Poisoning The best kept secret in the

1st Time only
C   G   /Bb   F   /C   G   /Bb   F   ://
west,   The

2nd Time
STOP
C   /
west   Is this a

BRIDGE

```
Am        G      /Am    G    /F      C    /G            /
Russian  conspiracy,   no it's just idiocy  Is this a Chinese burn
                                                        >
Am        G      /Am    G    /F      C    /G            /           /
I've got a dinosaur  for a   representative It's got a small brain and refuses      to learn
```

SOLO

```
Am              /G           /F      C    /G            /
Am              /            /G           /             /
Bb              /C           /Bb          /C            /
       Their promotion's so lame     They could never ever take it to the real ball game
                                             >
F    C    /G        /F     C    /G           /          /
Listen  I ain't a pet   Or a token hipster, in your monopoly set     You bet 'cause
```

CHORUS

```
C    G    /Bb   F   /C    G    /Bb    F    /
   I've got,  mercury poisoning  It's fatal and it don't get better

C    G    /Bb   F   /Bb              /
   I've got,  mercury poisoning The best kept secret in the
```

CHORUS OUTRO

```
C    G    /Bb   F   /C    G    /Bb    F    /
west (He's got),  mercury poisoning   It's fatal and it don't get better

C    G    /Bb   F   /Bb              /
   I've got,  mercury poisoning The best kept secret in the

C    G    /Bb   F   /C    G    /Bb    F    /
west (He's got)  mercury poisoning    It's fatal and it don't get better

C    G    /Bb   F   /Bb              /
   We've got,  mercury poisoning The best kept secret in the

C         /Bb            /C           /Bb           /
west  the best  the best kept secret in the west the best  the best kept secret in the

C         /Bb            /C           /Bb           /
west  the best  the best kept secret in the west the best  the best kept secret in the

C         /Bb            /C           /Bb           /
west  the best  the best kept secret in the west the best  the best kept secret in the
```

SINGLE CHORDS.....................
```
Am   G   /F   Bb   /C
```

MERCURY POISONING
GUITAR INTRO

I WANT YOU BACK (ALIVE!) 4/4

INTRO (with bar numbers)

```
1                   2               3                       4
Bb                  /Eb             /Gm  Bb/d  Eb  Bb  /Eb  Bbsus  Bb         /

5                       6                       7                   8
Bb  Dm  Gm  Gm7  /Eb  Bb/d  Cm7  F  /Gm  Gm7  Eb  Bb/d  /Cm7  F  Bb          /
```

VERSE 1 & 2

//:Bb   /Eb   /
   When I had you to myself, I didn't want you around   Those
   Tried to live without your love one of those sleepless nights

Gm   Bb/d   /Eb   Bbsus   Bb   /
pretty faces always make me stand up in a   crowd
But that just shows you girl,   that I know wrong from right

Bb   /Eb   /
Someone picked you from the bunch, and that was all it took
Every street you walk down,   I leave tear stains on the ground

Gm   Bb/d   /Eb   Bbsus   Bb   /
Now it's much too late for me to take a second look
Following   you girl   I can feel you all around. Let me tell ya now

CHORUS 1   1st time only

Bb Dm Gm Gm7   /Eb   Bb/d   Cm7   F   /
Oh   baby, give me one more chance   (show you that I love you)

Gm   Gm7 Eb   Bb/d /Cm7   F   Bb   /
Won't you please let   me   (back in your heart)

Bb Dm Gm Gm7   /Eb   Bb/d   Cm7   F   /
Oh   darlin', I was blind to let you go   (Let you go, baby)

Gm   Gm7 Eb   Bb/d /Cm7   F   Bb   /
Now   that   I   see   you in his arms (I want you back)

Bb   /   /
Oh I do now   (I want you back) Oh oh baby   (I want you back)
                              2/4
Bb   /   ://
Oh I do now   (I want you back) Oh oh baby

CHORUS 2

| Bb | Dm | Gm | Gm7 | /Eb | Bb/d | Cm7 | F | / |

Oh baby, give me one more chance (show you that I love you)

| Gm | Gm7 | Eb | Bb/d | /Cm7 | F | Bb | | / |

Won't you please let me (back in your heart)

| Bb | Dm | Gm | Gm7 | /Eb | Bb/d | Cm7 | F | / |

Oh darlin', I was blind to let you go (Let you go, baby)

| Gm | Gm7 | Eb | Bb/d | / |

Now that I see you

BRIDGE

| Bb | Dm | Cm | Bb | / Bb | Dm | Cm | Bb / | Bb | Dm | Cm | Bb / |

In his arms   oh yeah   oh

| Bb | Dm | Cm | Bb | /Bb | Dm | Cm | Bb /Bb | Dm | Cm | Bb / |

Yeah   oh oh oh oh oh   oh oh oh oh oh   oh oh oh

| Bb | Dm | Cm | Bb | / Bb | Dm | Cm | Bb /Bb | Dm | Cm | Bb / |

oh oh   You're all I want   You're all I want   You're all I

CHORUS 3

| Bb | Dm | Gm | Gm7 | /Eb | Bb/d | Cm7 | F | / |

Need   Oh yeah   one more chance (show you that I love you)

| Gm | Gm7 | Eb | Bb/d | /Cm7 | F | Bb | | / |

Won't you please let me (back in your heart)

| Bb | Dm | Gm | Gm7 | /Eb | Bb/d | Cm7 | F | / |

Oh darlin', I was blind to let you go (Let you go, baby)

| Gm | Gm7 | Eb | Bb/d | /Cm7 | F | Bb | | / |

Now that I see you in his arms

CHORUS 3 (continued)

```
                               2/4
Bb                    /             /
(Forget what happened then) and let me live a-

4/4
Bb   Dm  Gm   Gm7   /Eb   Bb/d   Cm7    F    /
gain      oh yeah         one more chance

Gm   Gm7  Eb   Bb/d  /Cm7  F    Bb         /
Baby (baby) baby (baby) baby (baby!)
                               2/4
Bb                    /             /
(Forget about the cost)   and give back what I
```

CHORUS 4

```
4/4
Bb   Dm  Gm   Gm7   /Eb   Bb/d   Cm7    F    /
Lost      oh yeah         one more chance (show you that I love you)

Gm   Gm7  Eb   Bb/d  /Cm7  F    Bb         /
Won't you  please let   me       (back in your heart)

Bb   Dm  Gm   Gm7   /Eb   Bb/d   Cm7    F    /
Oh   darlin', I was  blind to let you go    (Let you go, baby)

Gm   Gm7  Eb   Bb/d  /Cm7  F    Bb         /
Now  that  I    see   you   in his arms let me tell ya baby

Gm   Gm7  Eb   Bb/d  /Cm7  F    Bb         /
Now  that  I    see   you   in his arms

Bb                    /                       //
Oh I do now  (I want you back) Oh oh baby    (I want you back)
```

I WANT YOU BACK (ALIVE)
ELECTRIC GUITARS

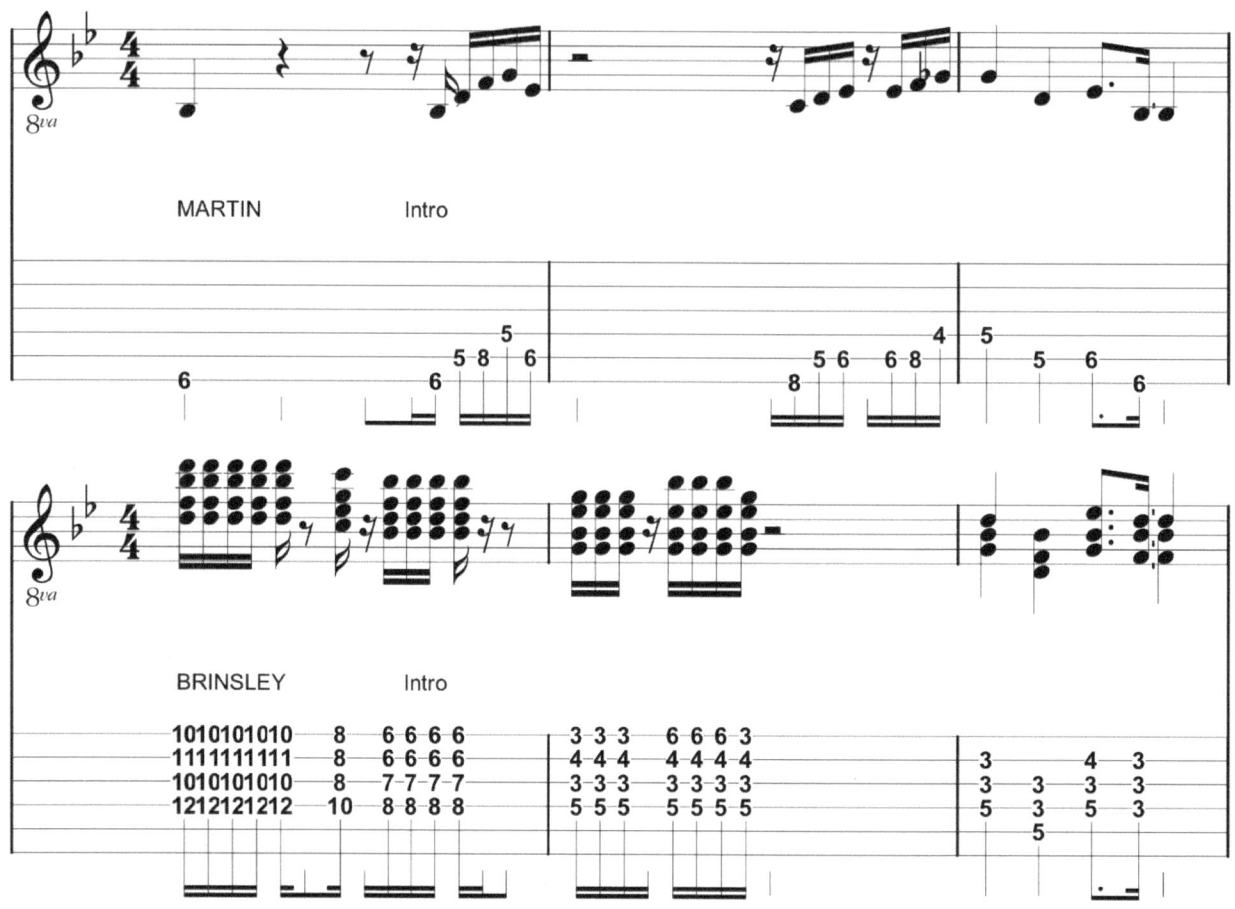

I WANT YOU BACK (ALIVE)
ELECTRIC GUITARS -

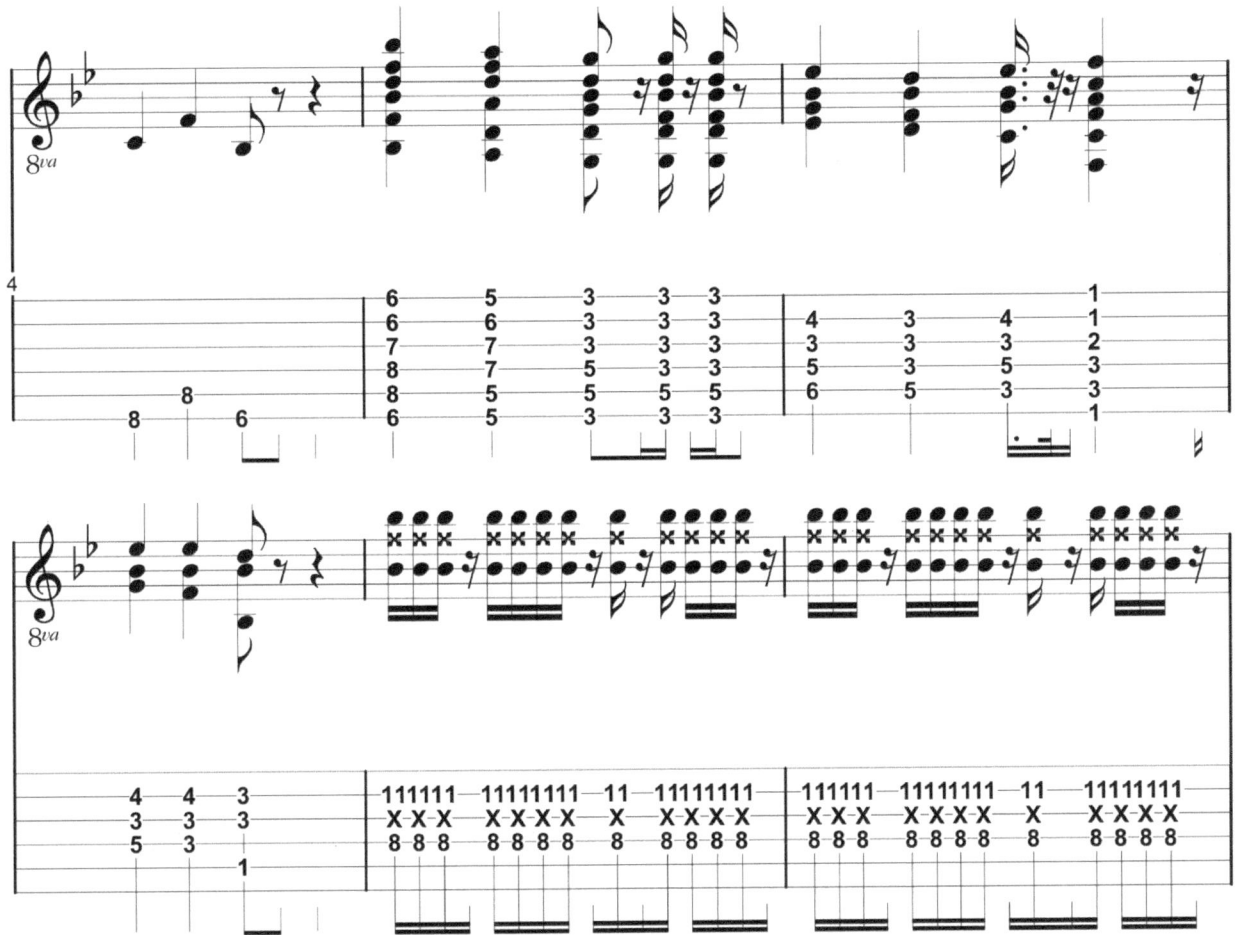

I WANT YOU BACK (ALIVE)
ELECTRIC GUITARS -

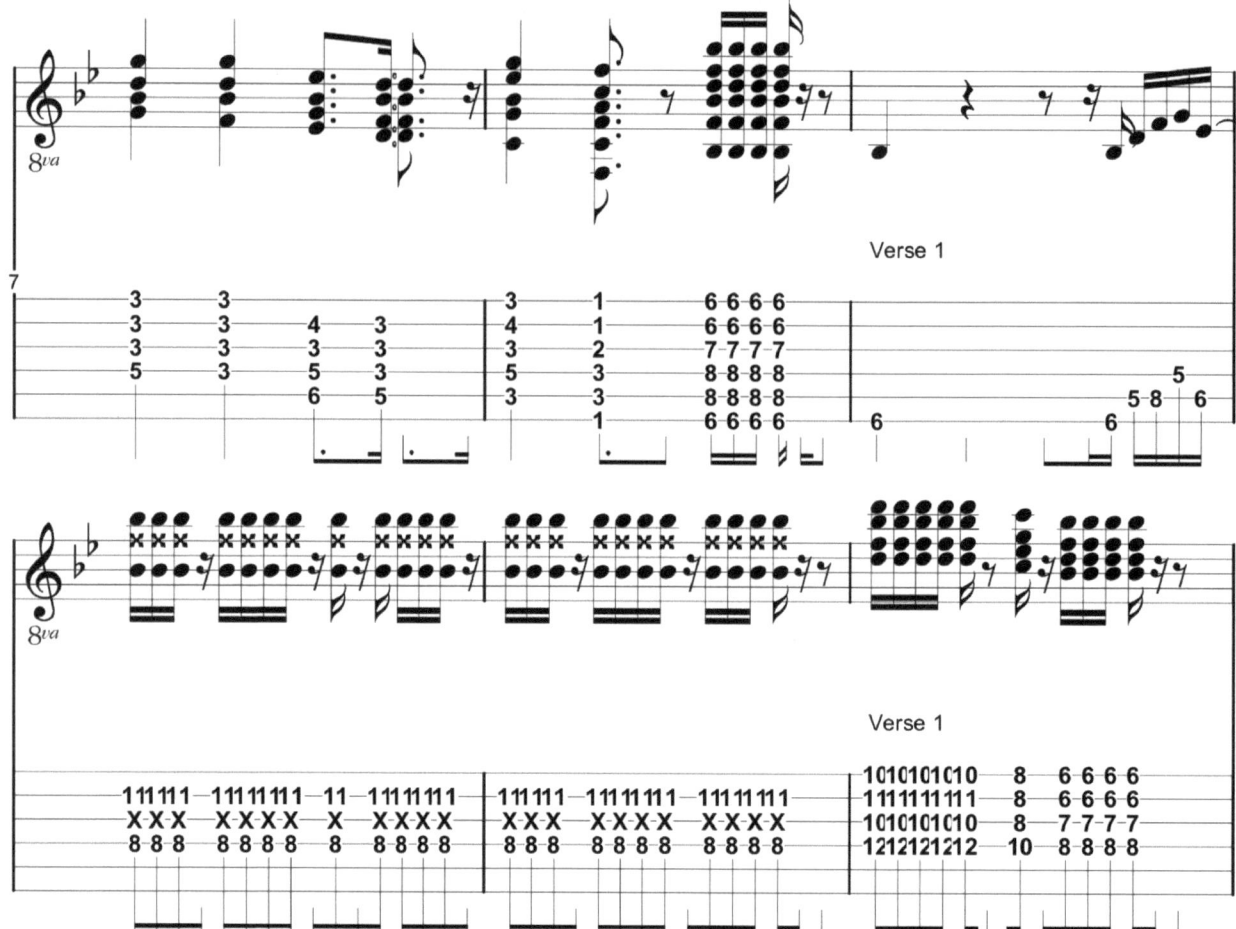

I WANT YOU BACK (ALIVE)
ELECTRIC GUITARS -

I WANT YOU BACK (ALIVE)
ELECTRIC GUITARS -

I WANT YOU BACK (ALIVE)
ELECTRIC GUITARS -

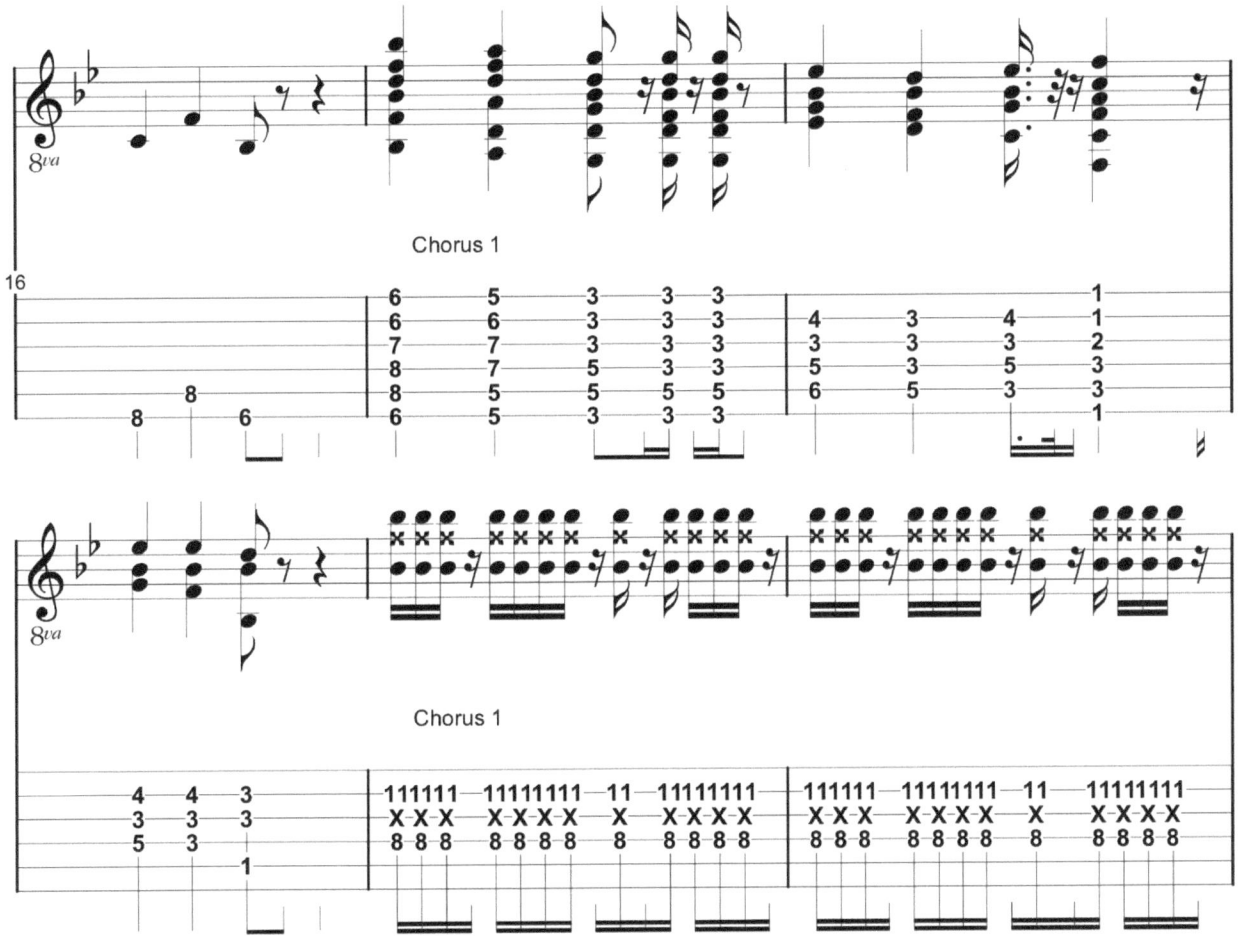

I WANT YOU BACK (ALIVE)
ELECTRIC GUITARS -

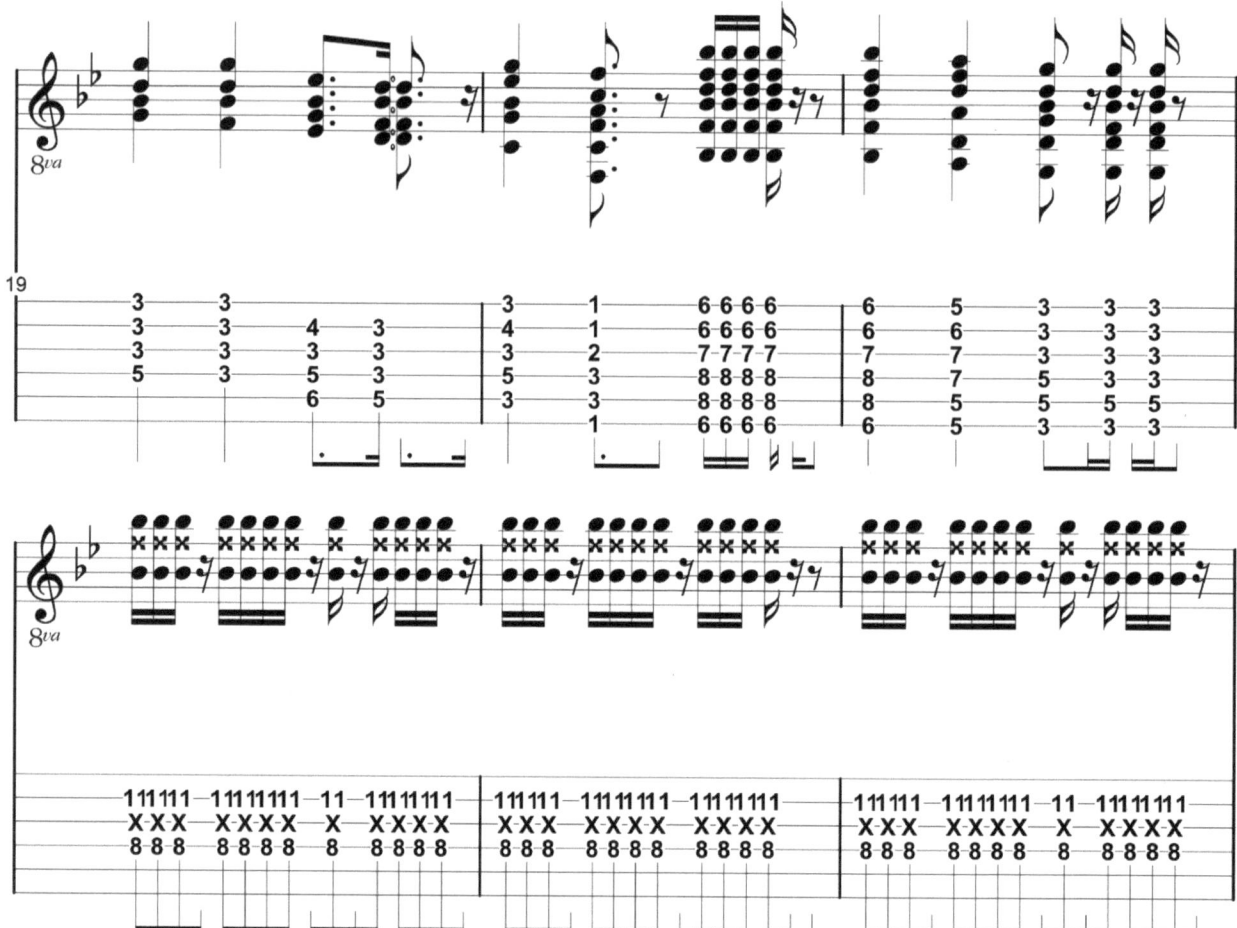

I WANT YOU BACK (ALIVE)
ELECTRIC GUITARS -

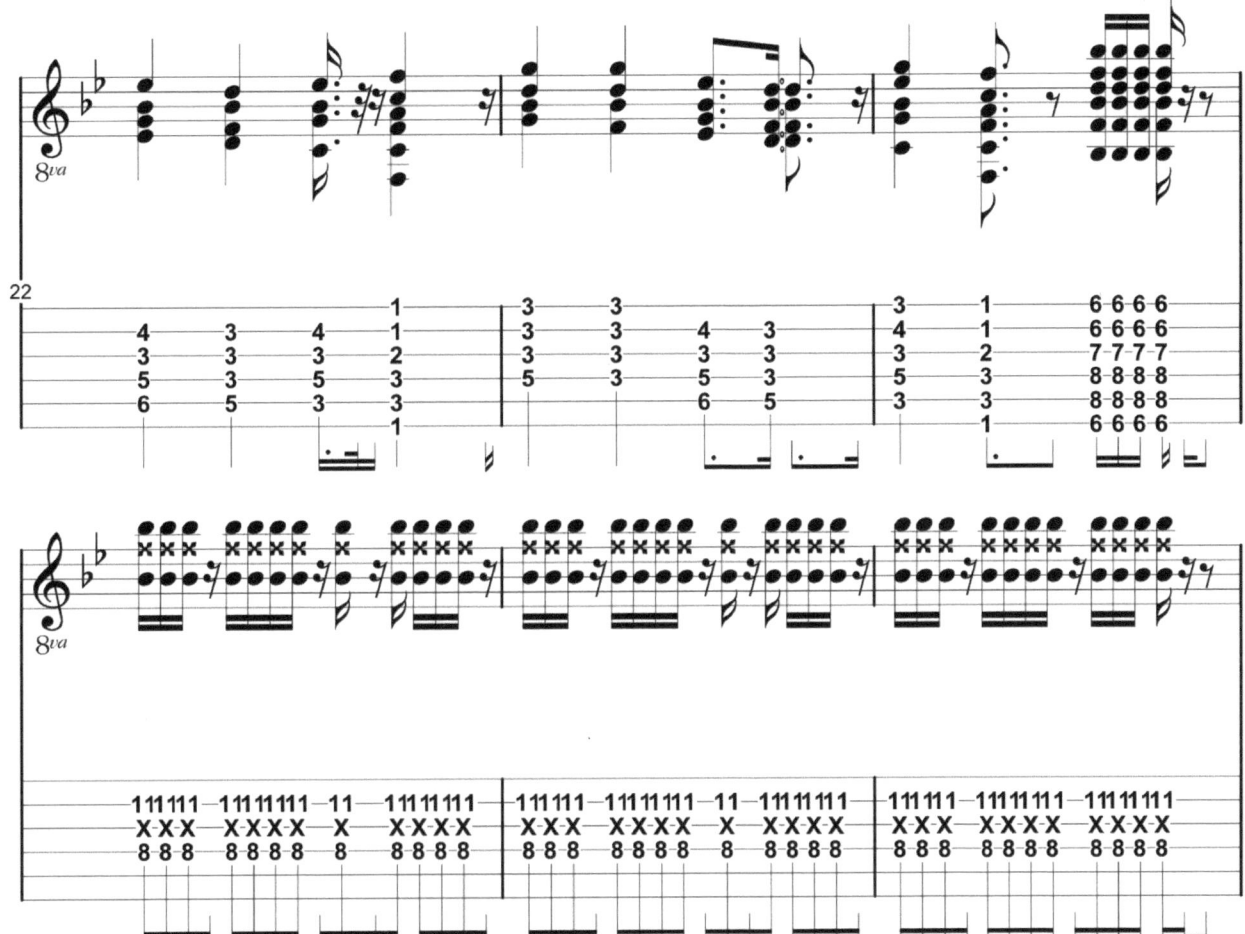

I WANT YOU BACK (ALIVE)
ELECTRIC GUITARS -

I WANT YOU BACK (ALIVE)
ELECTRIC GUITARS -

I WANT YOU BACK (ALIVE)
ELECTRIC GUITARS -

I WANT YOU BACK (ALIVE)
ELECTRIC GUITARS -

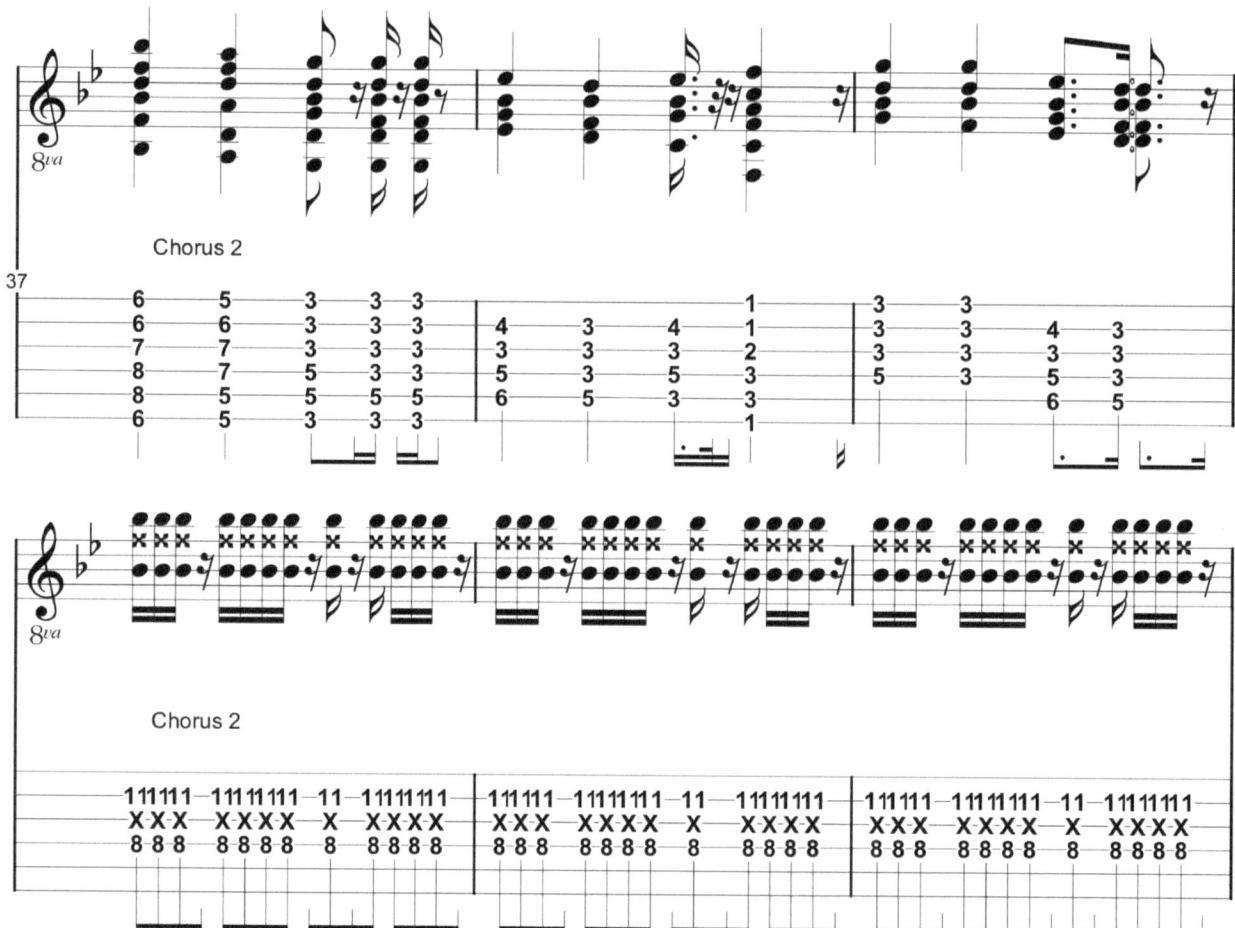

I WANT YOU BACK (ALIVE)
ELECTRIC GUITARS -

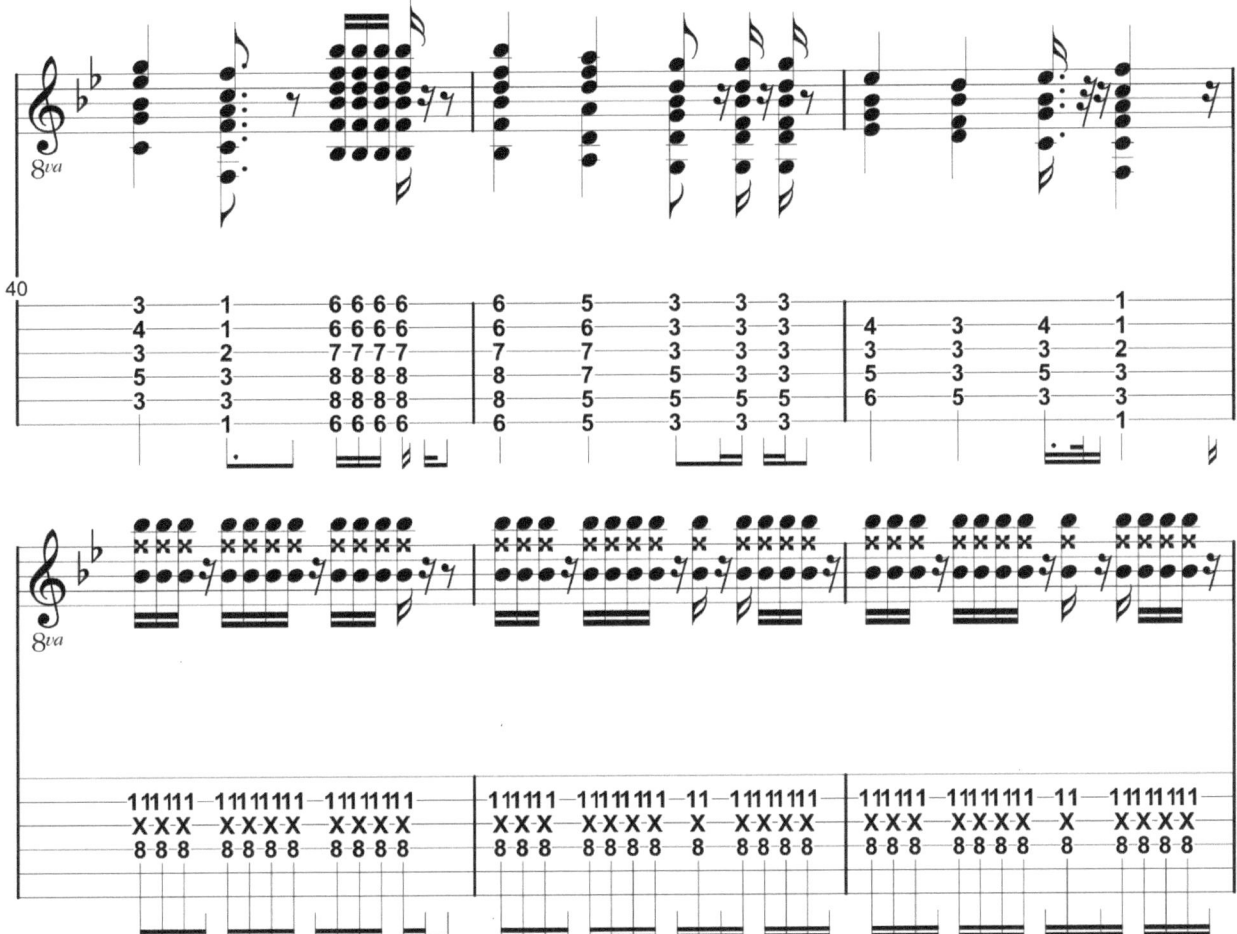

I WANT YOU BACK (ALIVE)
ELECTRIC GUITARS -

I WANT YOU BACK (ALIVE)
ELECTRIC GUITARS -

I WANT YOU BACK (ALIVE)
ELECTRIC GUITARS -

I WANT YOU BACK (ALIVE)
ELECTRIC GUITARS -

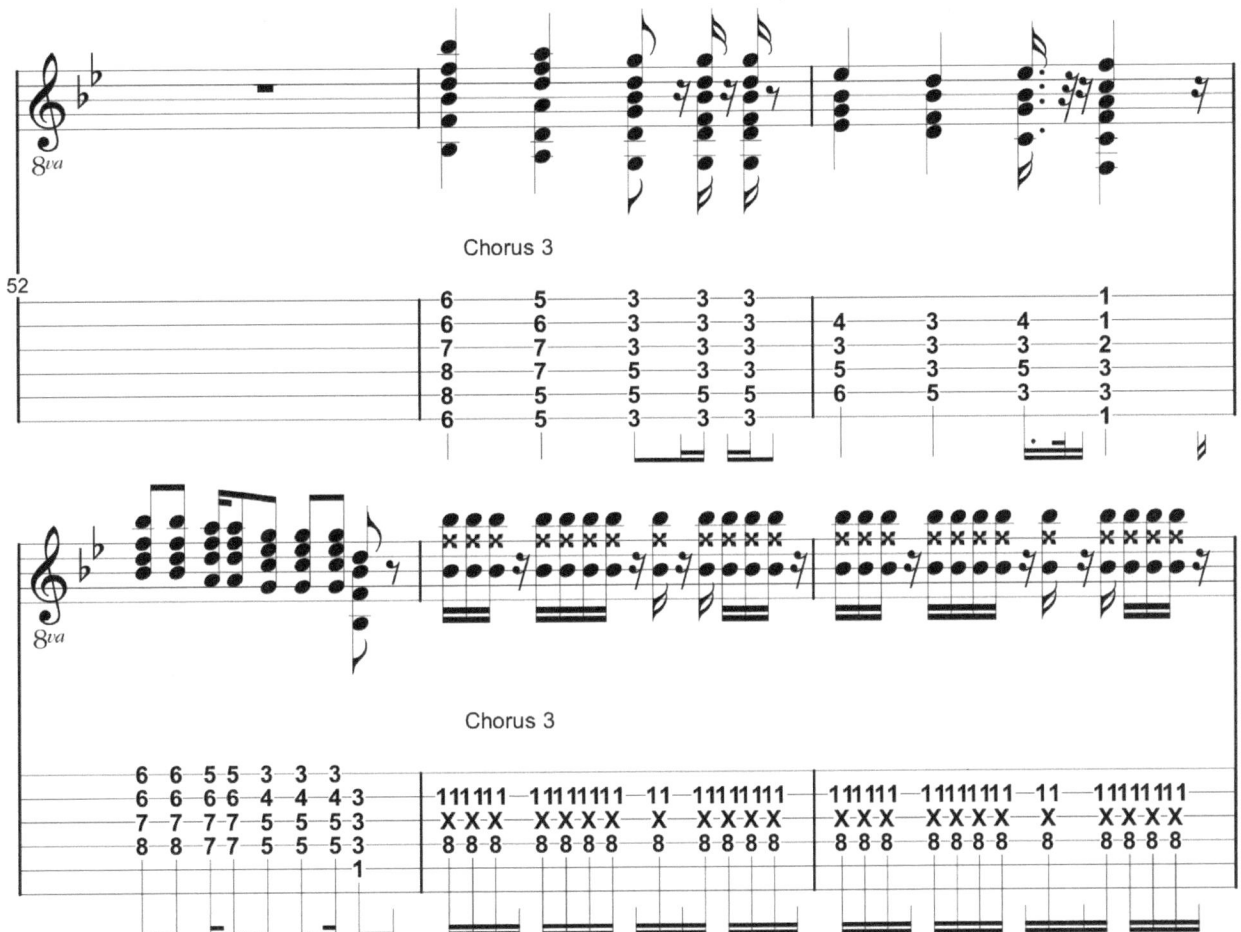

I WANT YOU BACK (ALIVE)
ELECTRIC GUITARS -

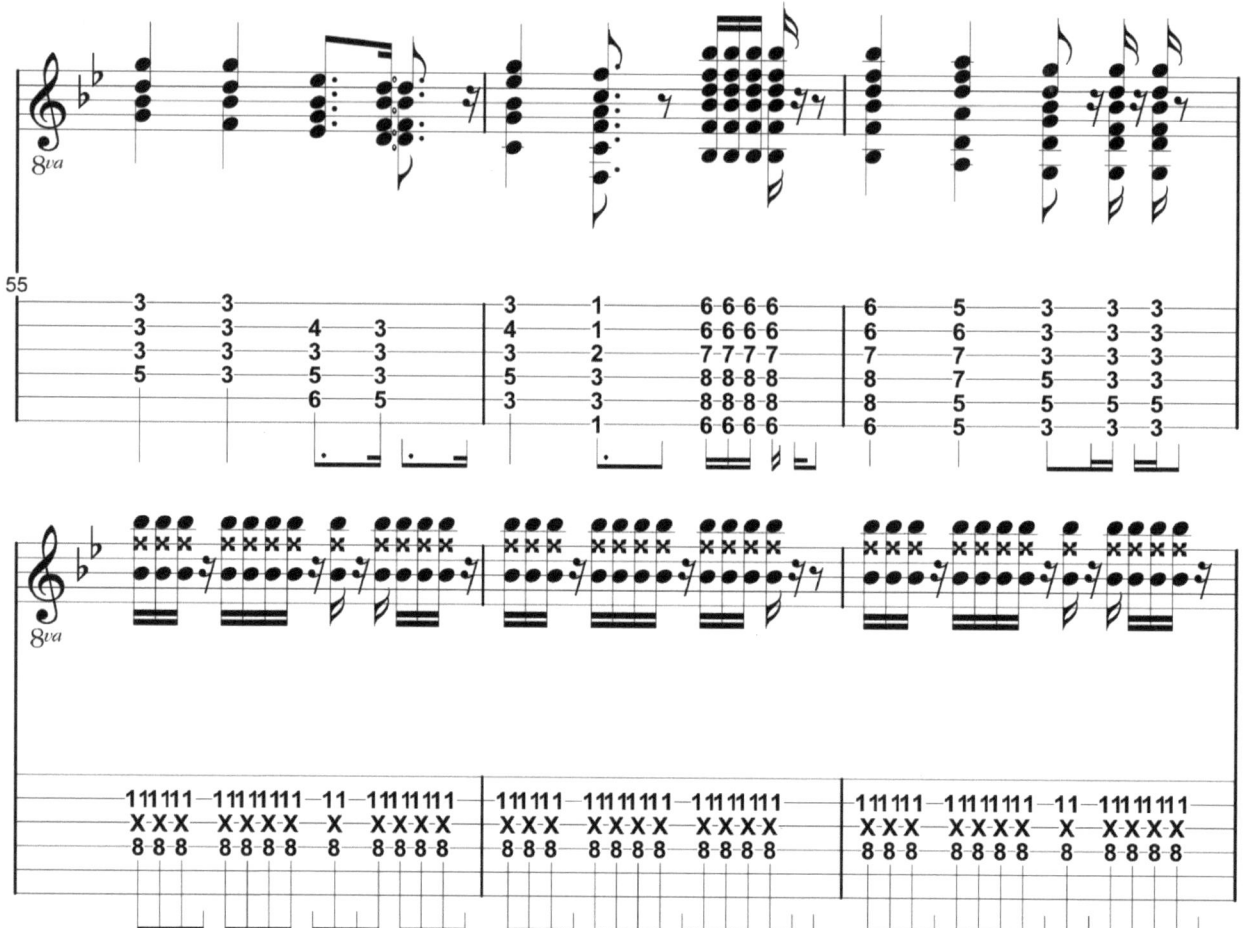

I WANT YOU BACK (ALIVE)
ELECTRIC GUITARS -

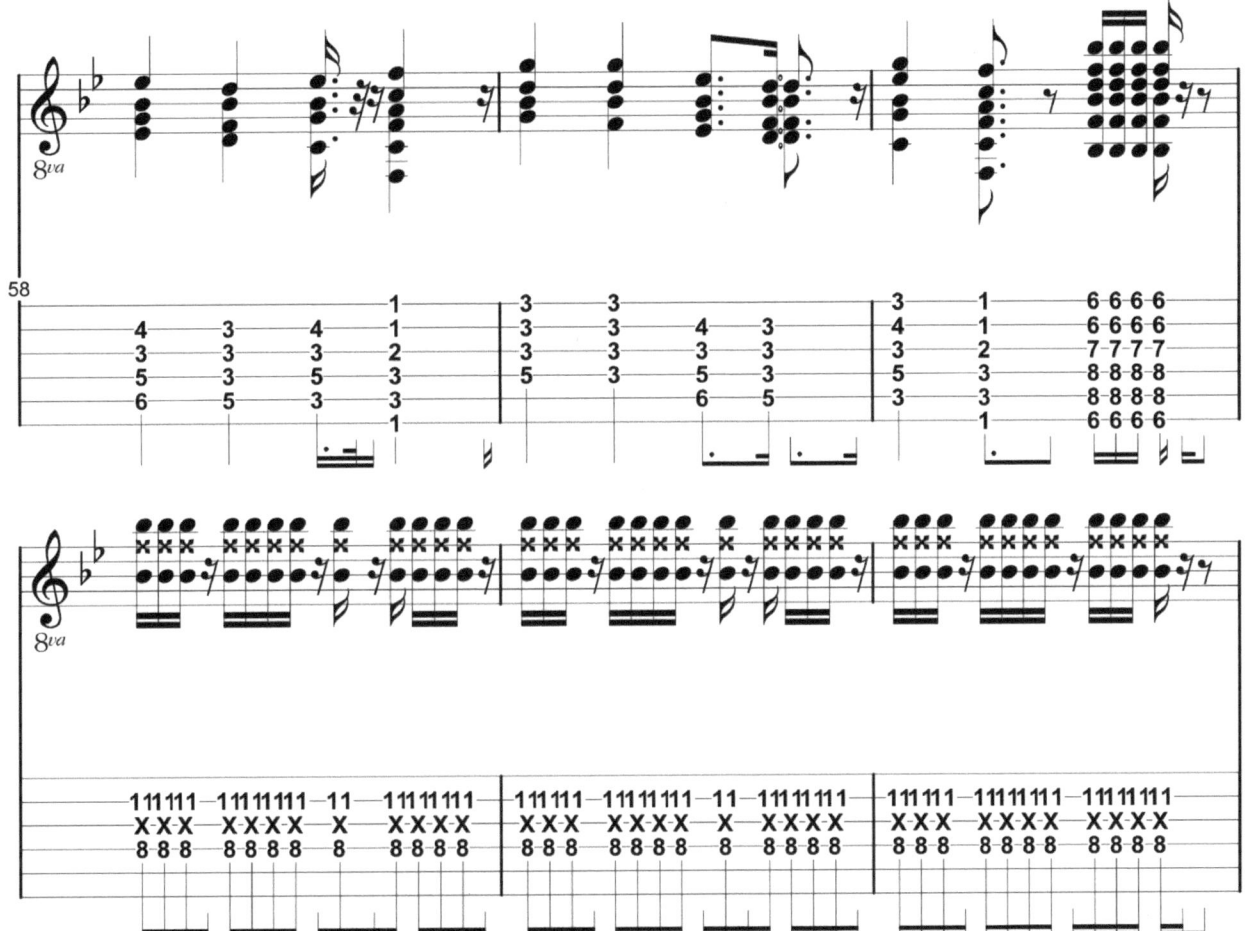

I WANT YOU BACK (ALIVE)
ELECTRIC GUITARS -

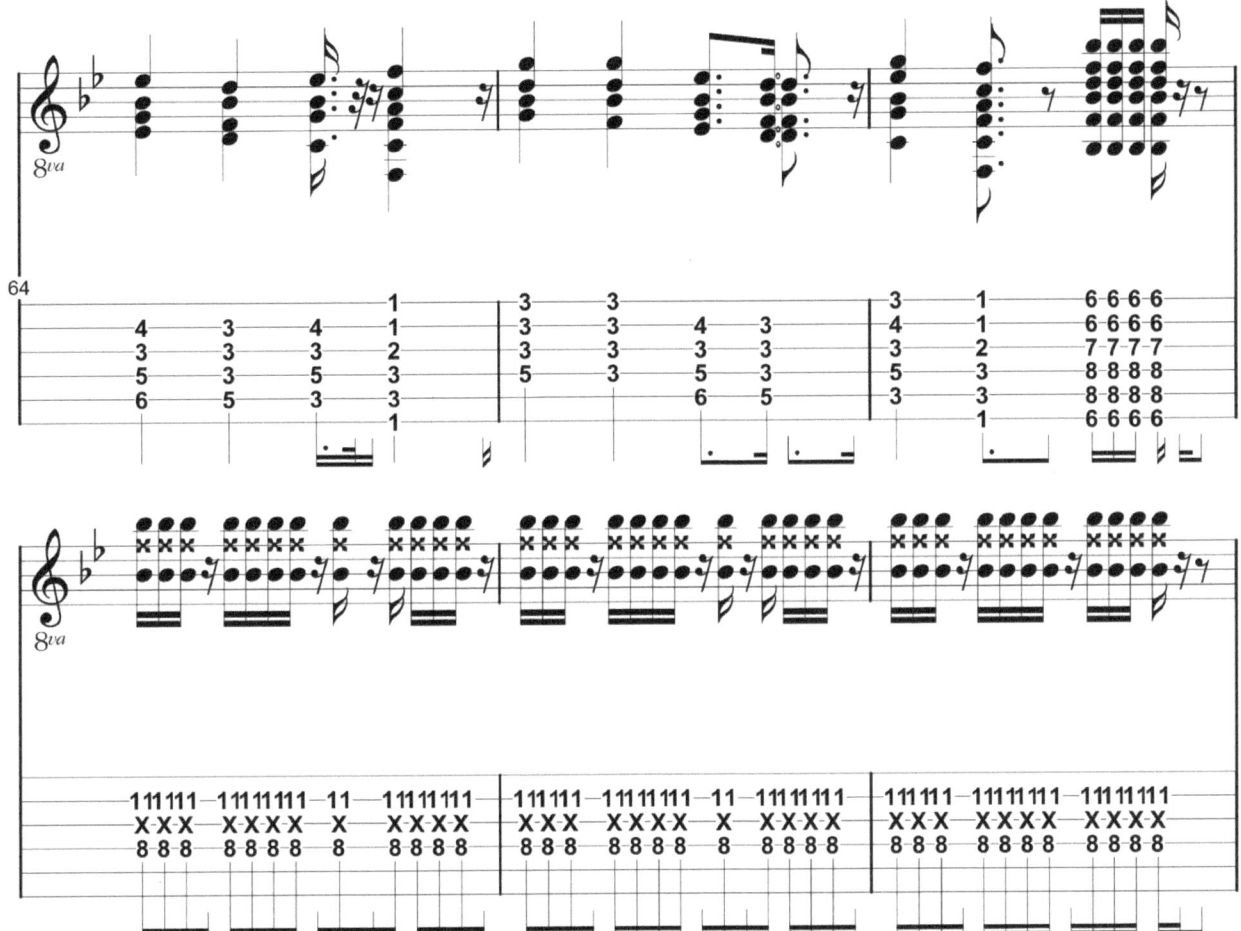

I WANT YOU BACK (ALIVE)
ELECTRIC GUITARS -

I WANT YOU BACK (ALIVE)
ELECTRIC GUITARS -

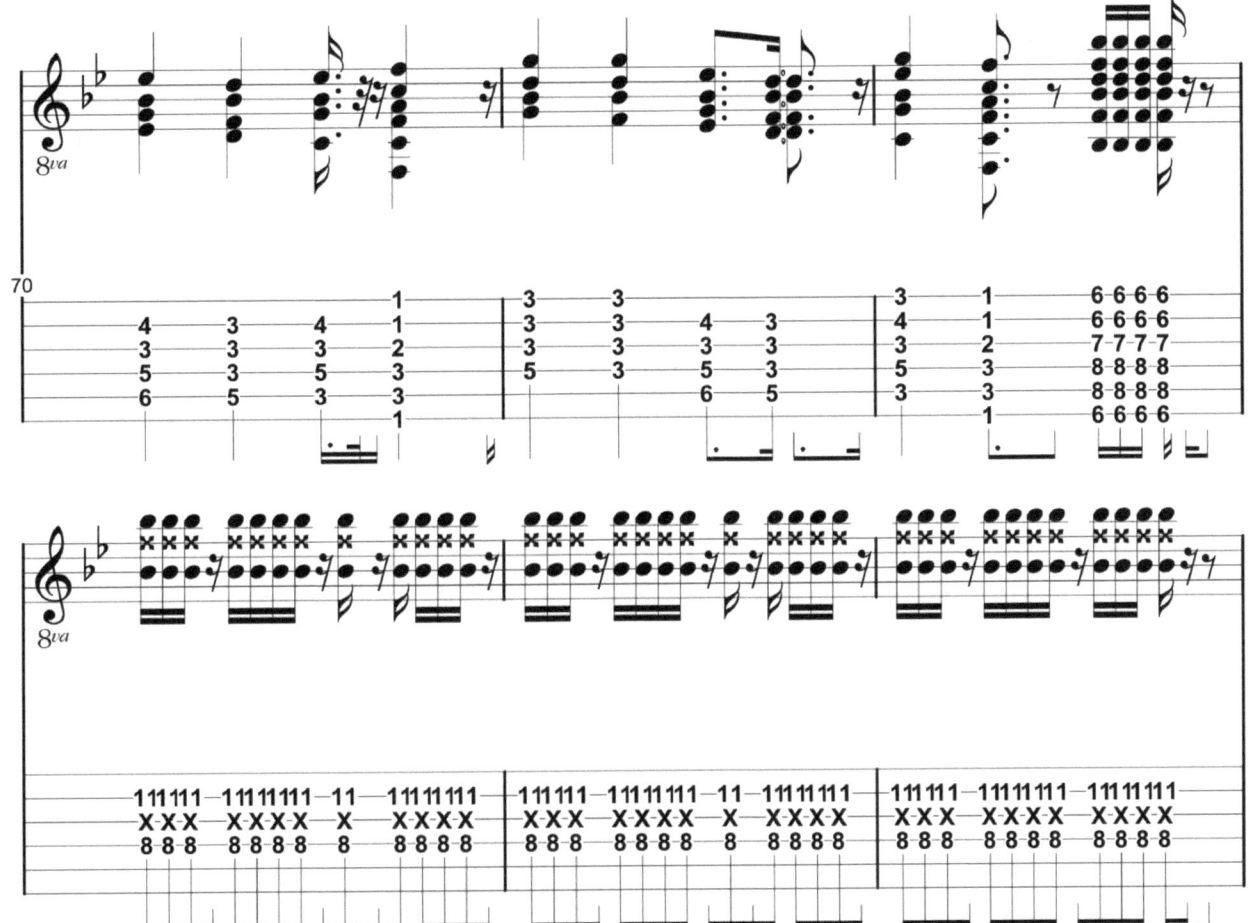

I WANT YOU BACK (ALIVE)
ELECTRIC GUITARS -

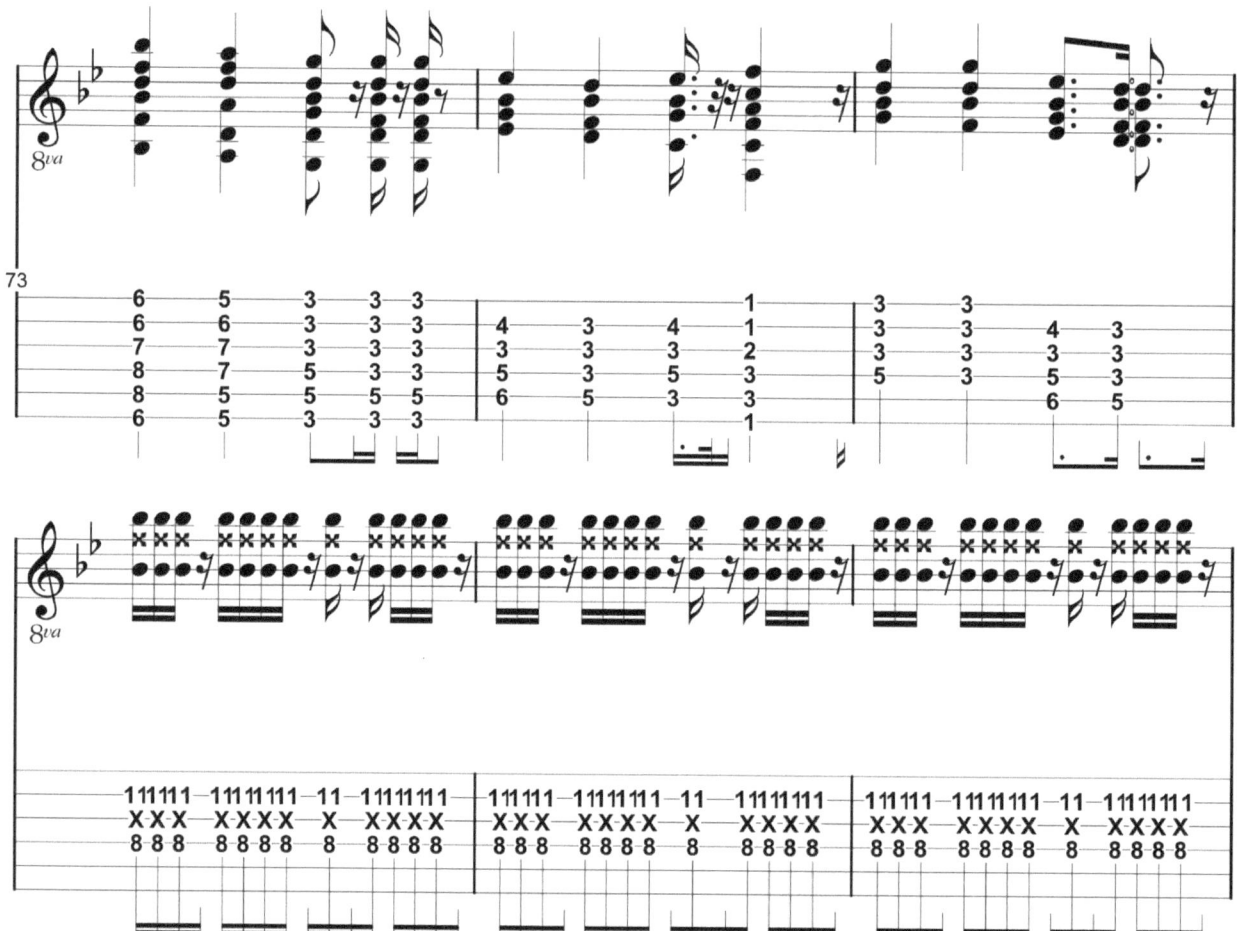

I WANT YOU BACK (ALIVE)
ELECTRIC GUITARS -

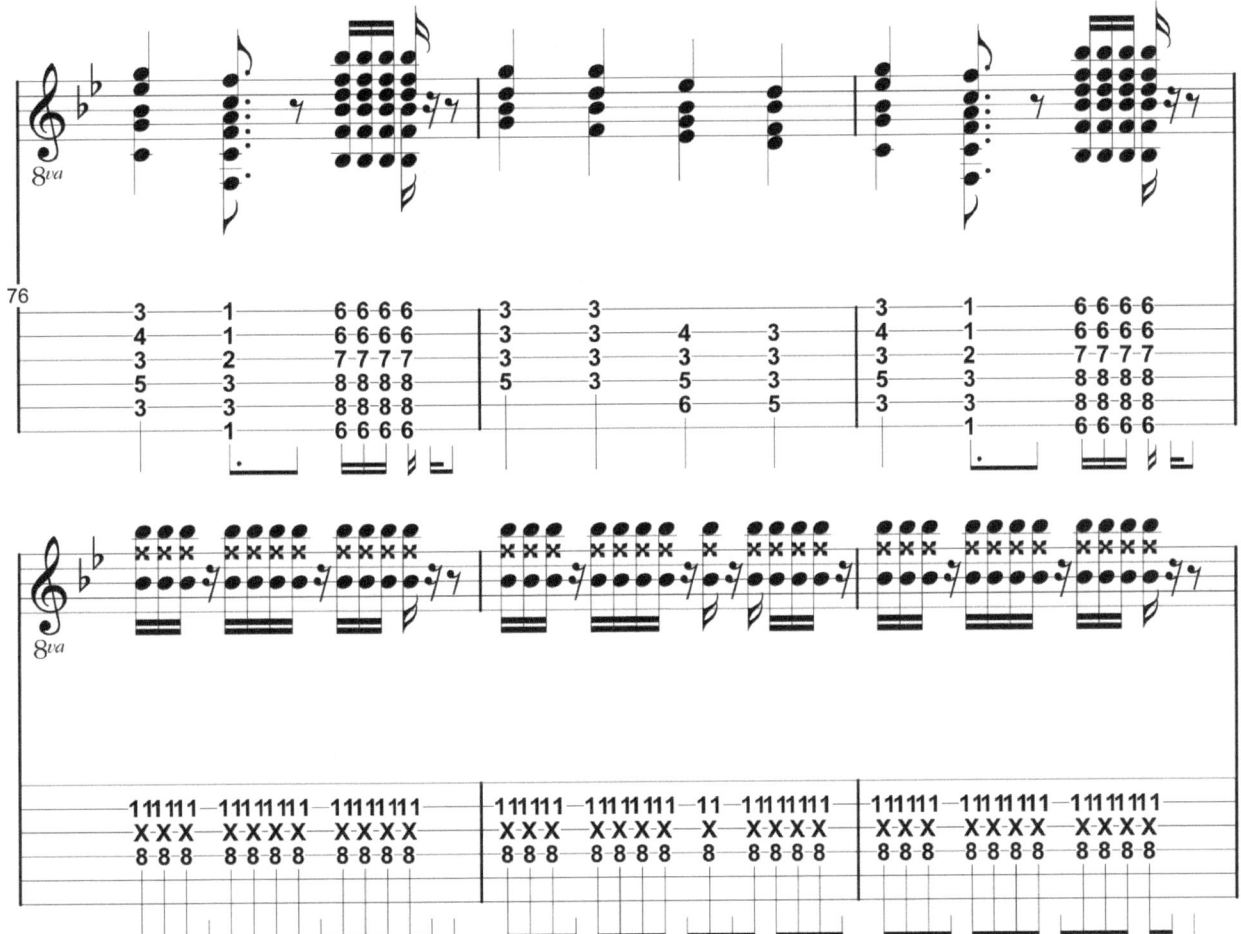

I WANT YOU BACK (ALIVE)
ELECTRIC GUITARS -

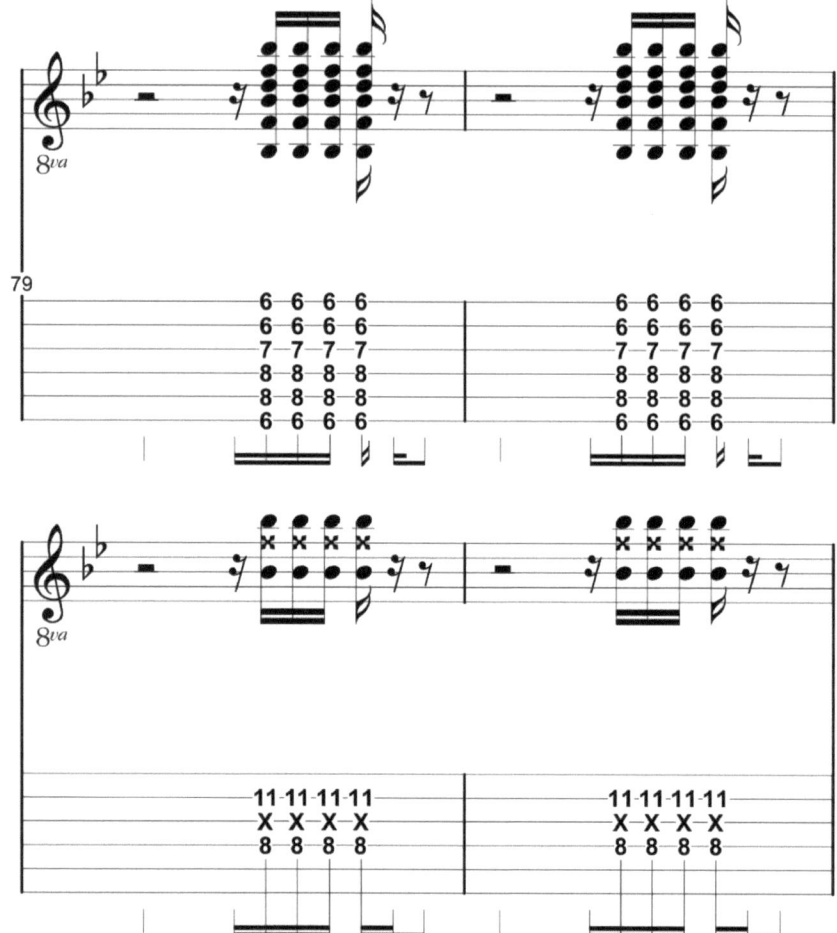

Left to right (top): Bob Andrews, Pat Andrews, Martin Belmont, Steve Goulding

Left to right (bottom): Jolie Parker, Graham Parker, Alan Frey, Andrew Bodnar

ACKNOWLEDGMENTS

I would like to thank Graham and Brinsley for their contributions. I would also like to thank Jay Nachman, Sheva Golkow, and Will Birch for providing me with some of the materials used in this book.

A big thanks to John Howells for turning the sheets of music, words and tablature that I typed on my computer, into an actual songbook!

And thanks to Jimmy for his fabulous cover design.

ABOUT THE AUTHOR

Martin Belmont started playing guitar for a living in 1972. His first full time band was Ducks Deluxe. He was one of the founder members of The Rumour who met up with Graham Parker in 1975. They recorded 6 albums and toured the UK (many times), Europe (many times), the USA (many times), Australia and New Zealand (twice) and Japan. They stopped working together in 1980.

Martin played with Carlene Carter, Nick Lowe, Paul Carrack, Elvis Costello (two tours as last minute substitute) Hank Wangford, My Darling Clementine, Reg Meuross and many sessions and one off gigs with artists as varied as Desmond Decker, Johnny Cash, Carl Perkins (playing on the same stage and standing next to George Harrison).

30 years after last working together, Graham asked the members of The Rumour to join him in Woodstock NY to record what turned out to be Three Chords Good. Later that year of 2011, The Rumour spent a week in Hollywood playing themselves in the Judd Apatow movie 'This is 40'. Three US tours, three UK tours, one with a short trip to Europe followed and in 2014 the album 'Mystery Glue' was recorded at RAK studios in London. After the final gigs in 2015 Martin compiled the 'Songs of Three Chords Good and Mystery Glue' and after consulting with his book writing partner John Howells they thought a Squeezing Out Sparks songbook to coincide with the 40th anniversary of that album's release would be a good idea. And here we are.

ALSO AVAILABLE

www.ingramcontent.com/pod-product-compliance
Lightning Source LLC
Chambersburg PA
CBHW041111070526
44584CB00002B/132